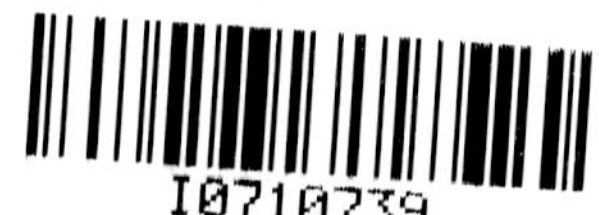

This Book Belongs to

....

....

....

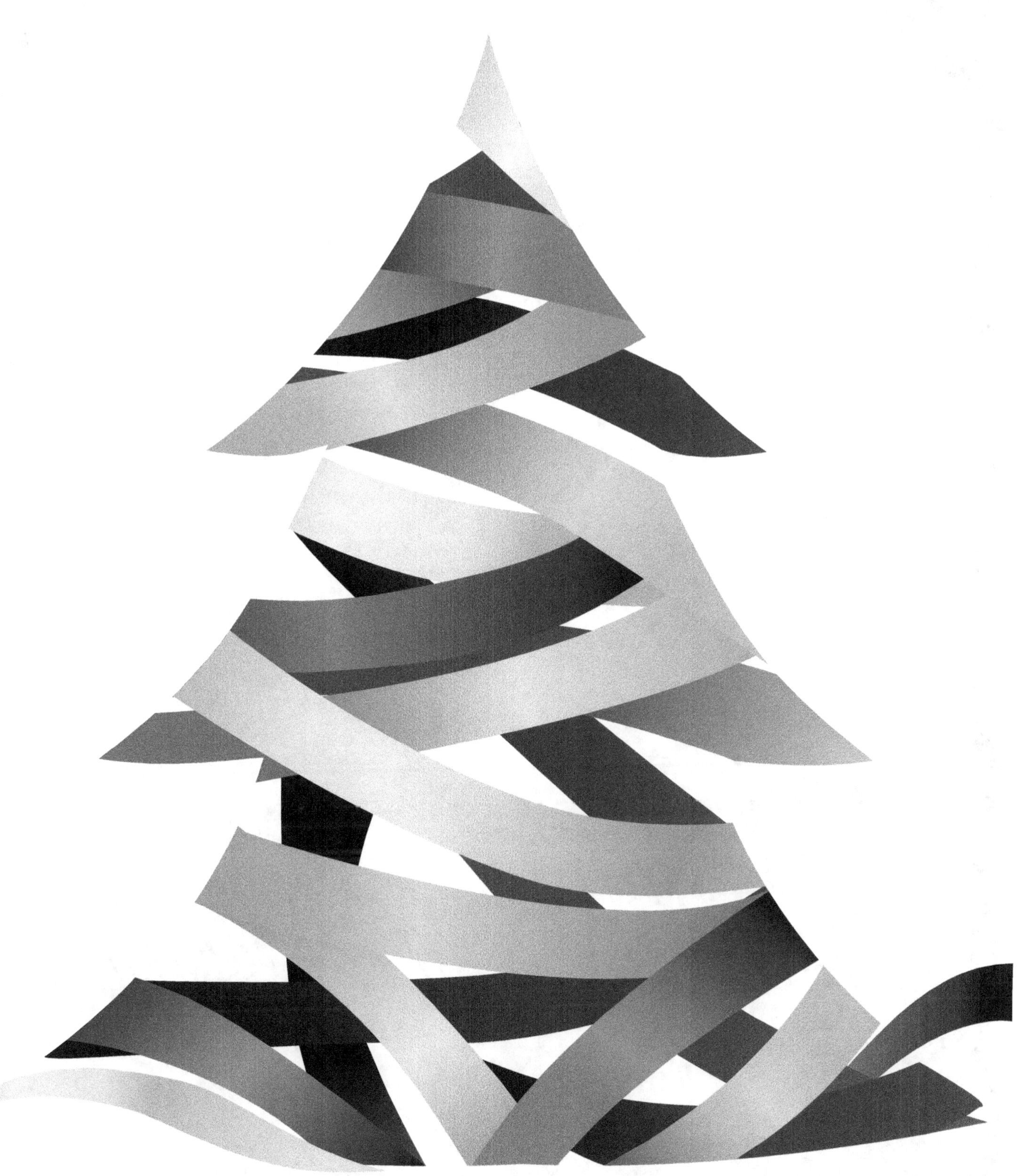

MERRY CHRISTMAS

Color Test

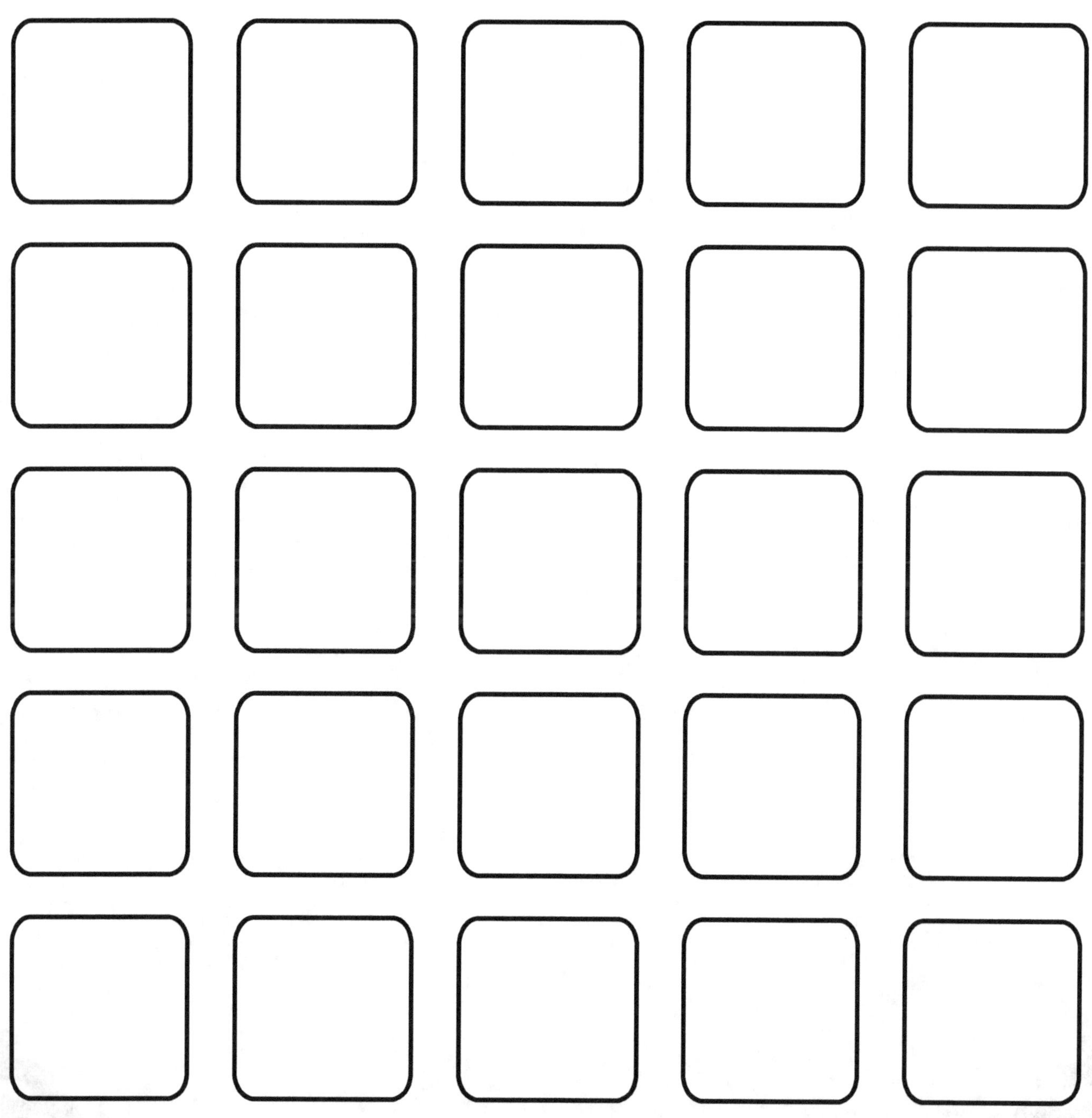

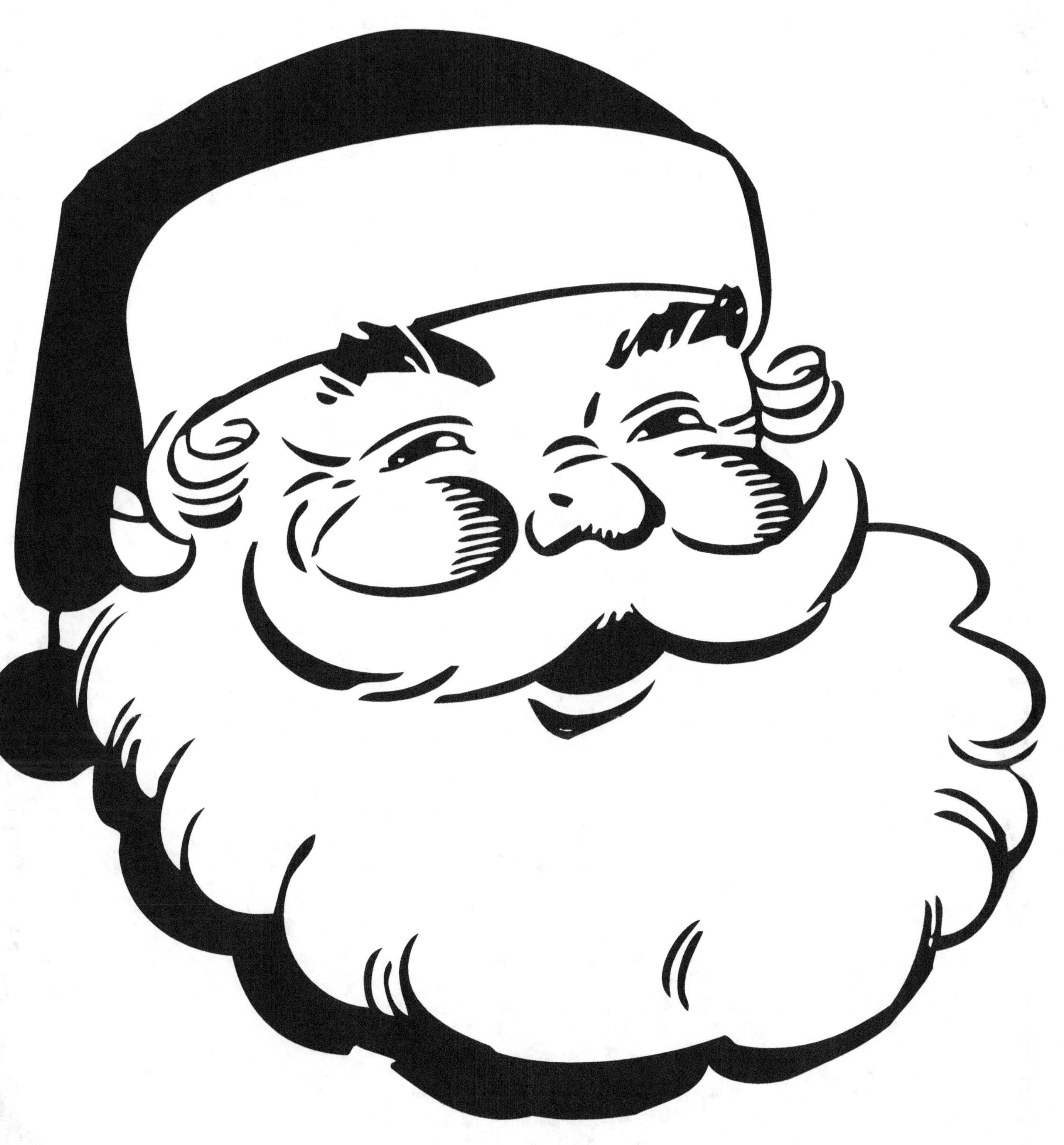

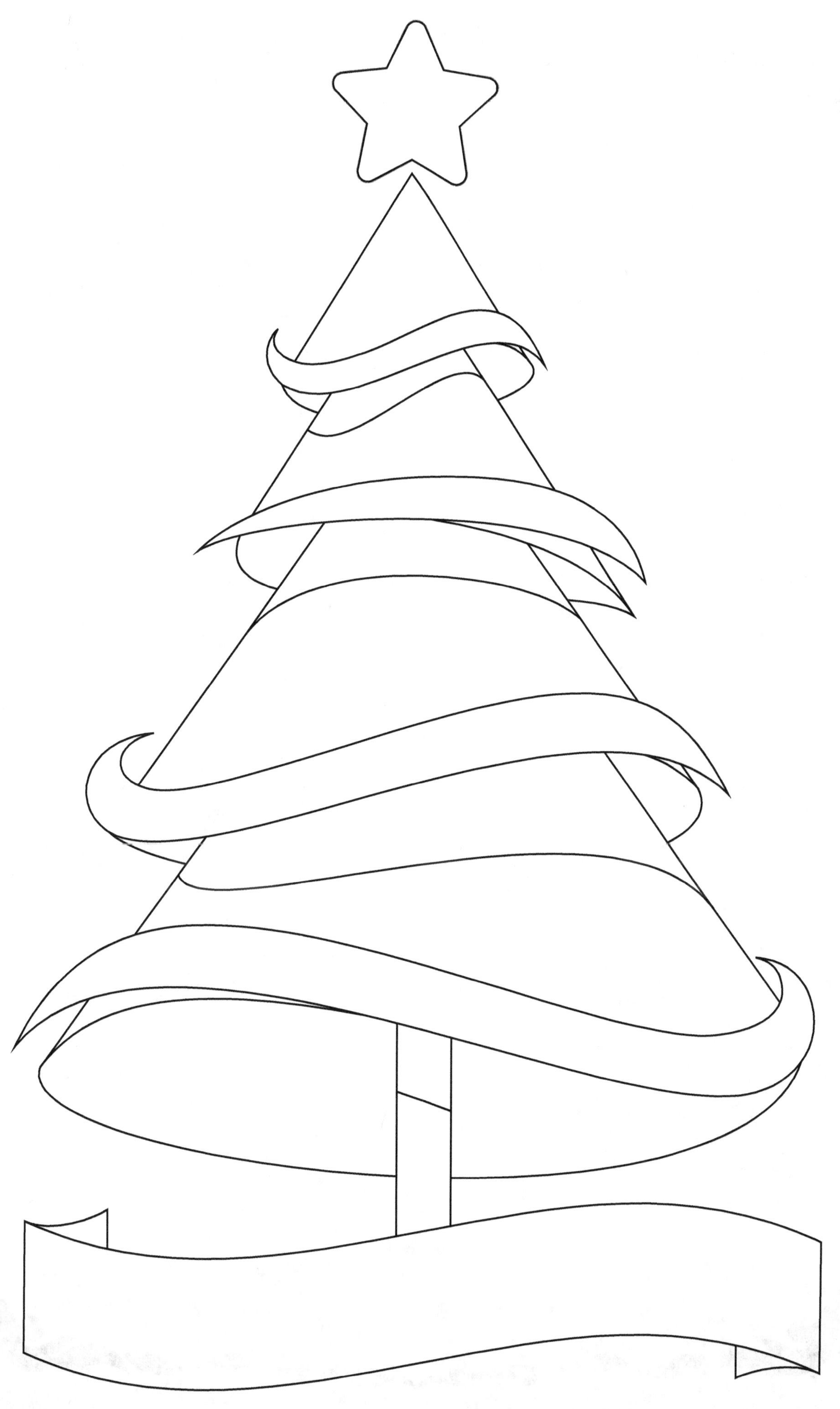

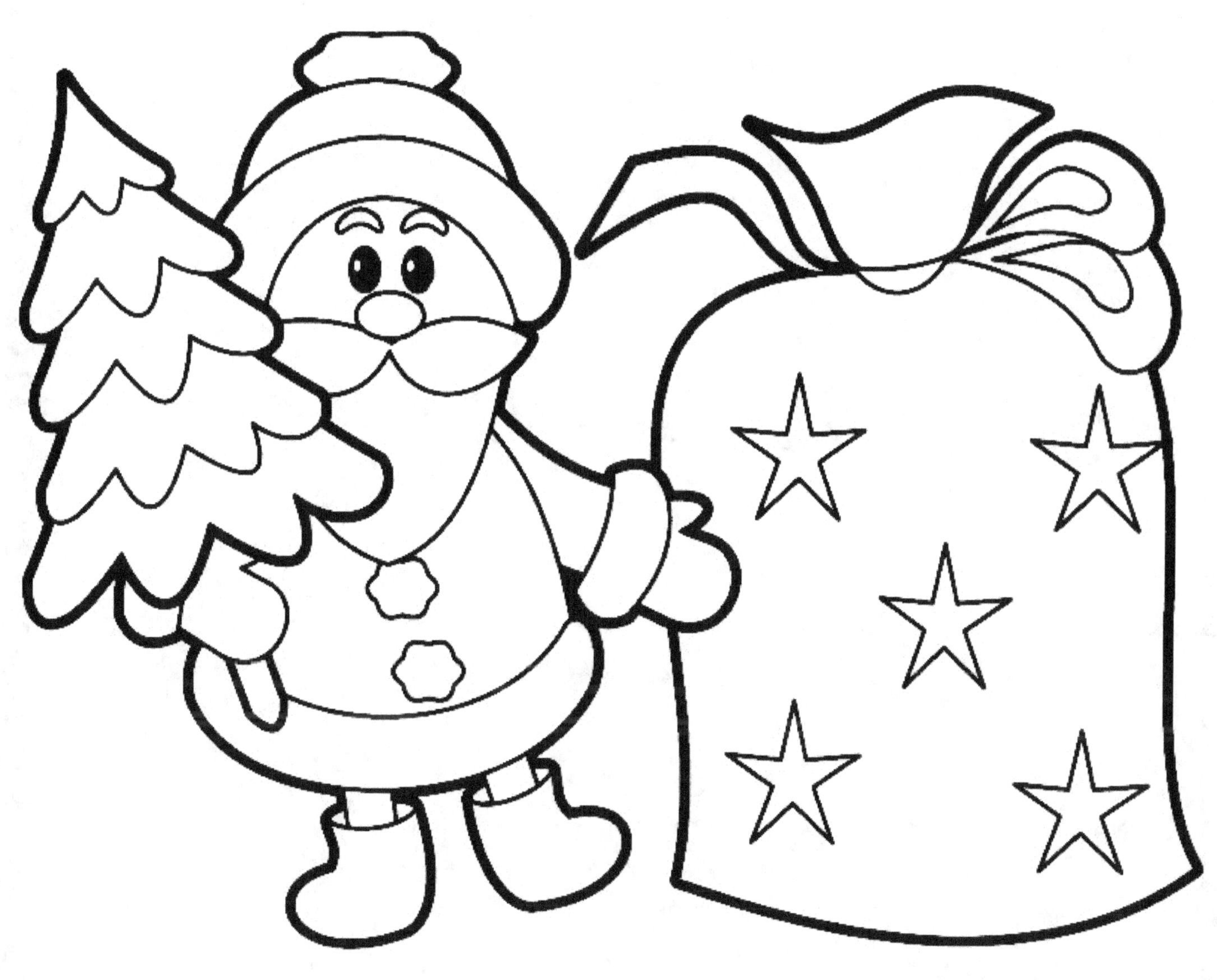

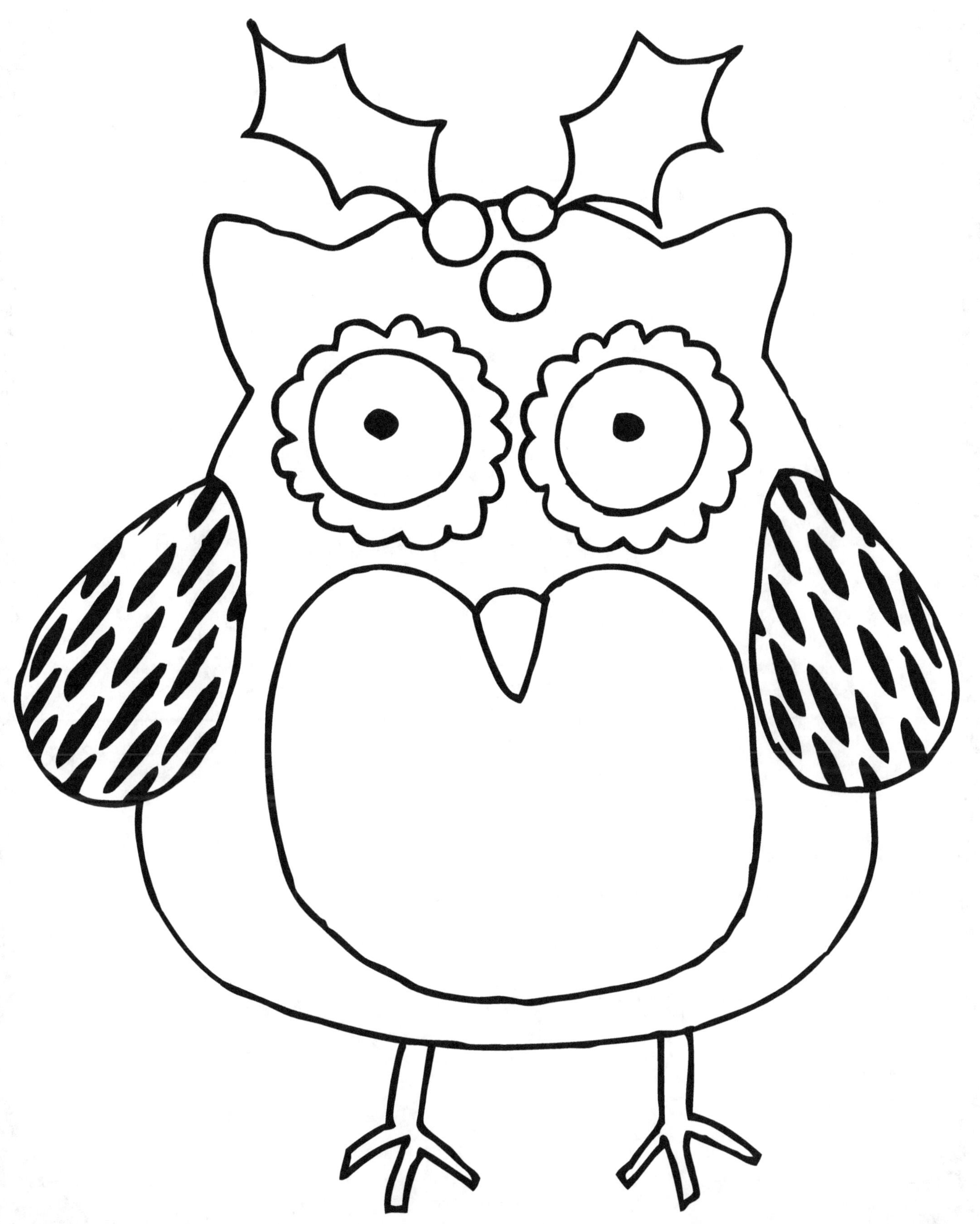

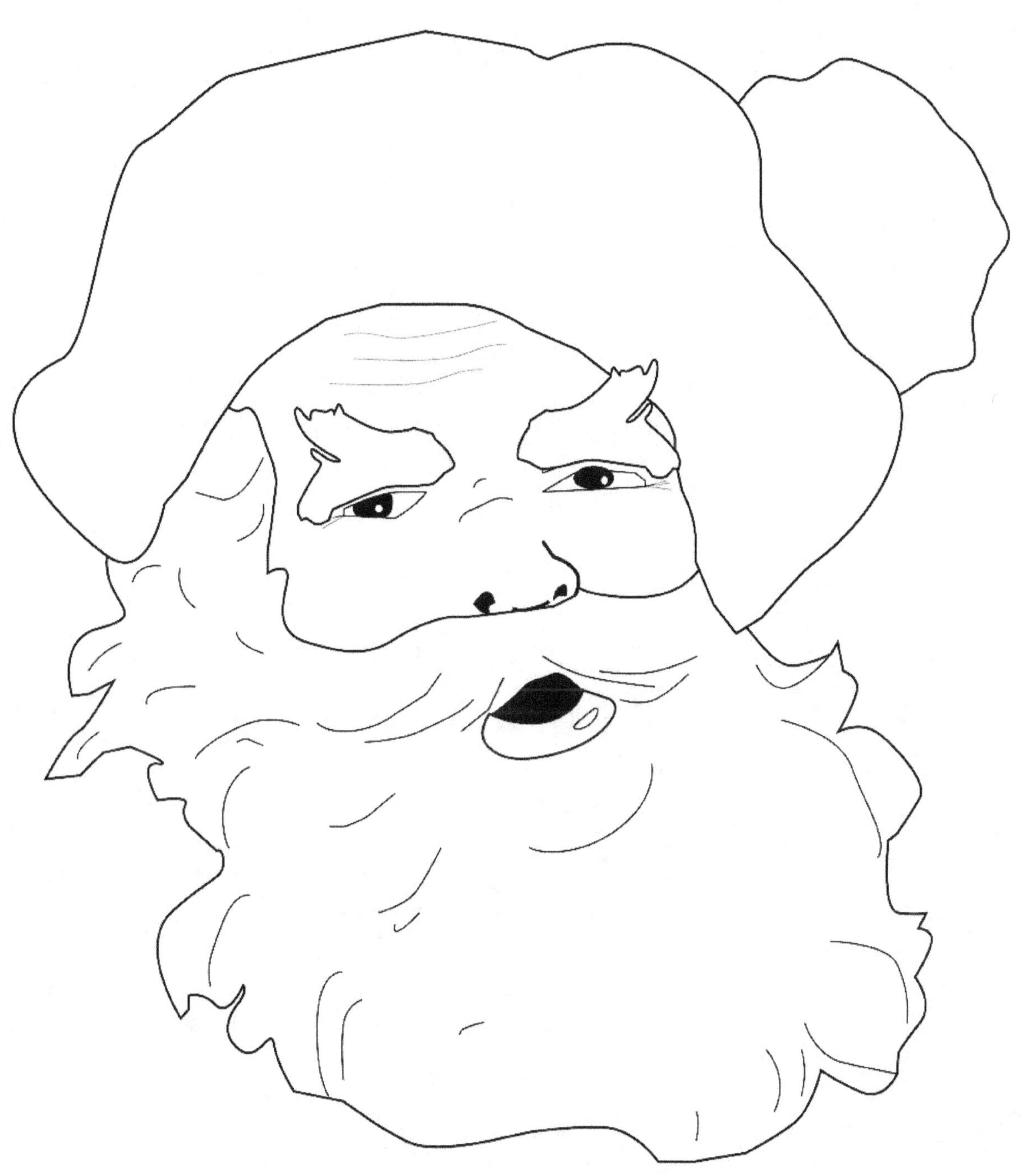

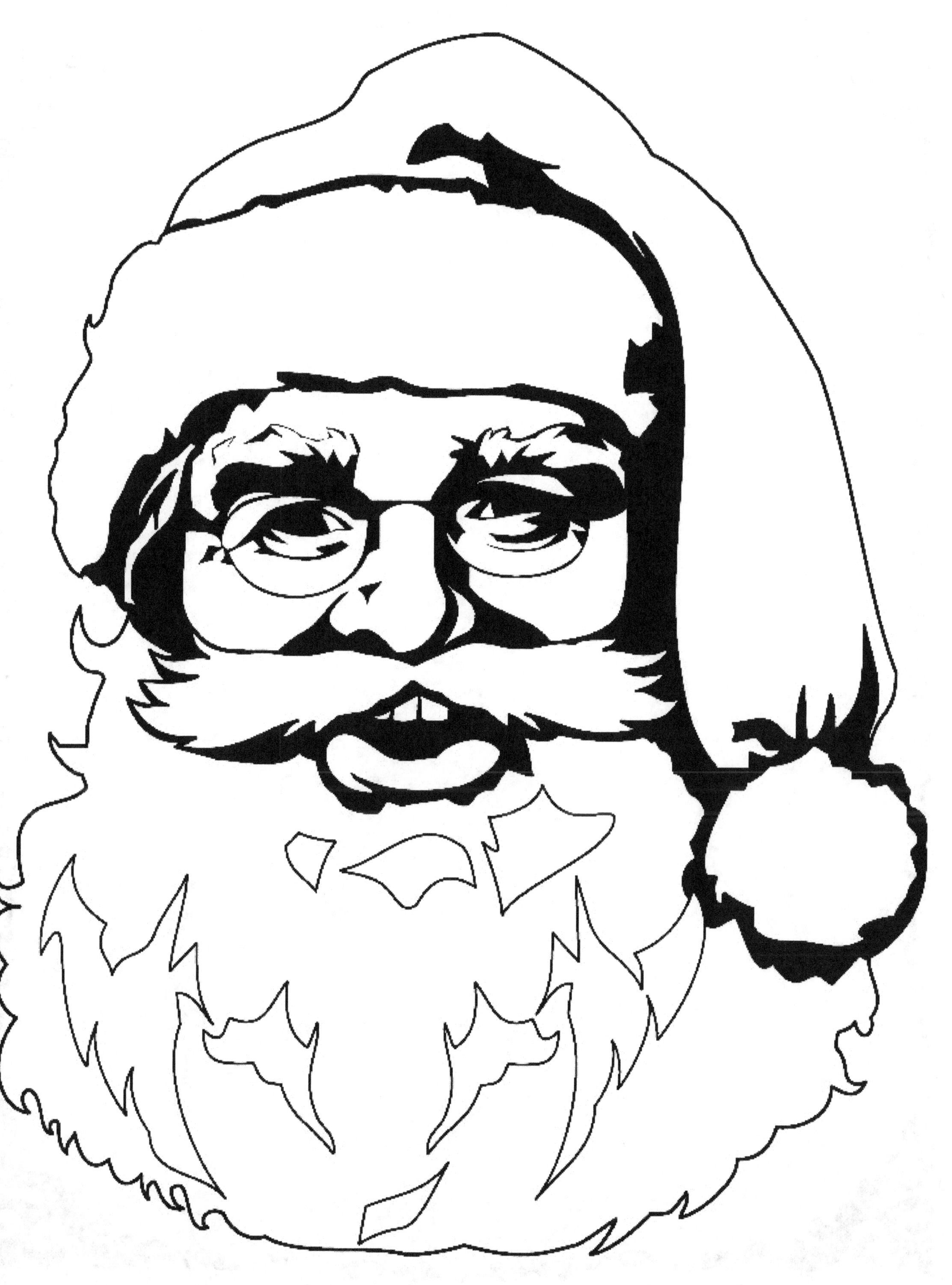

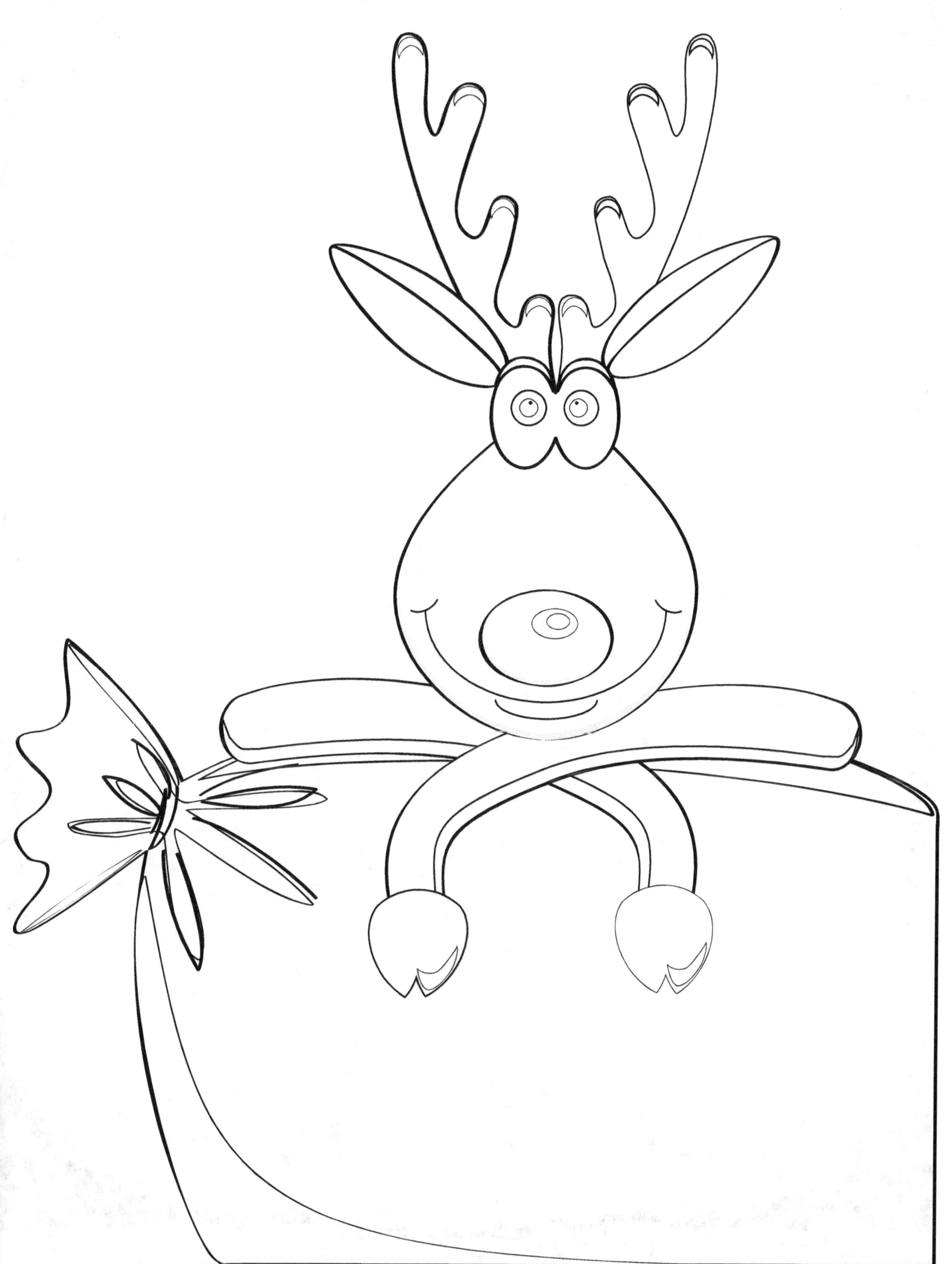

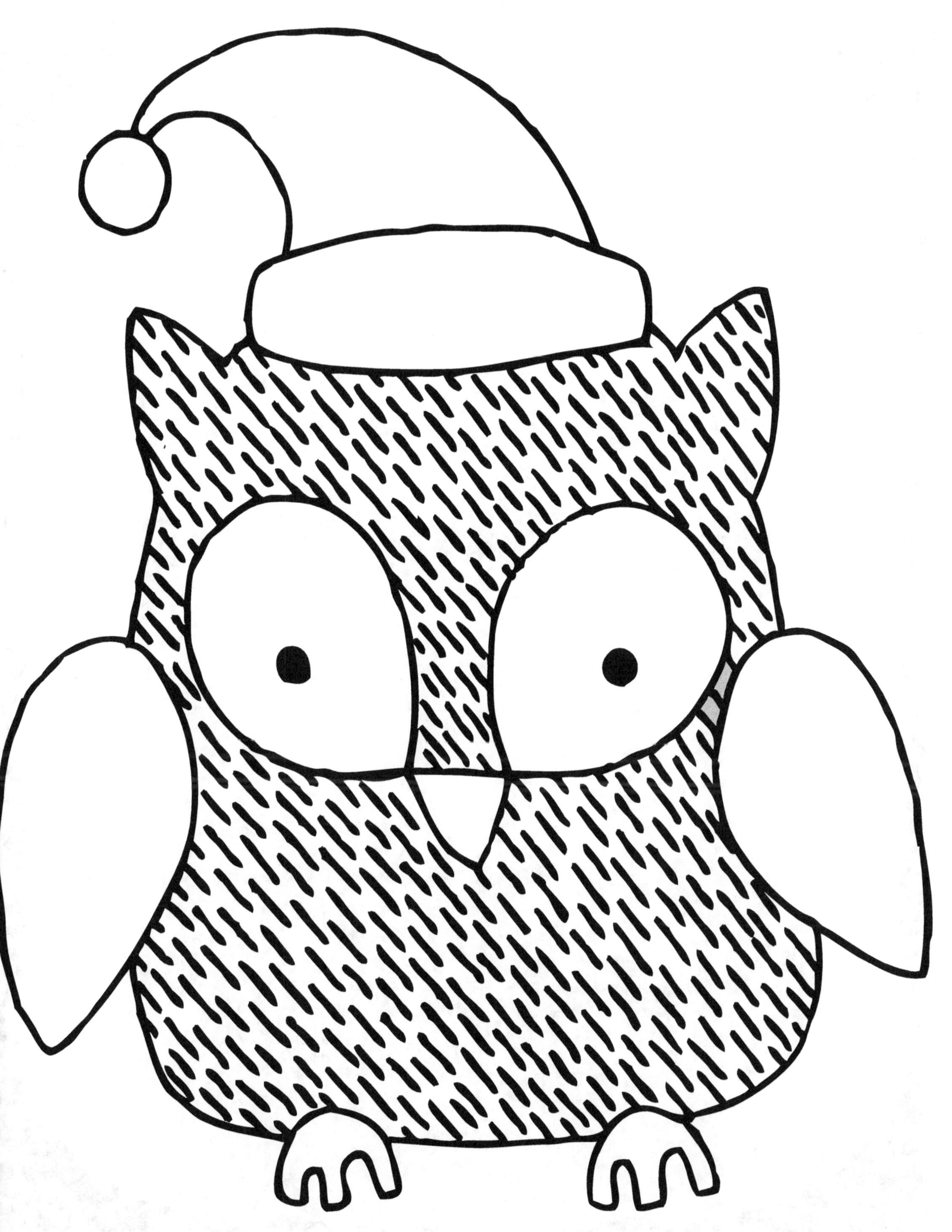

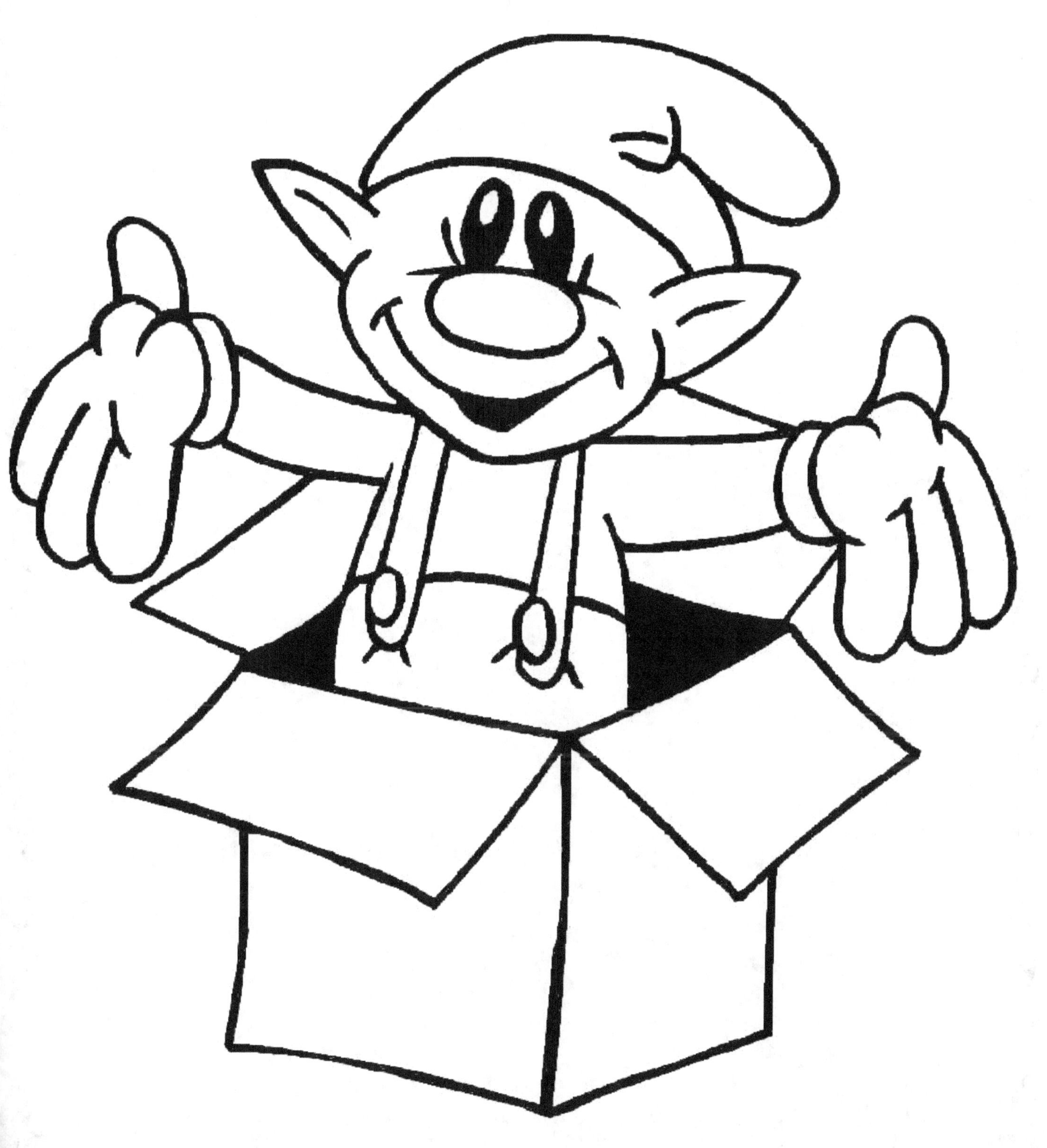

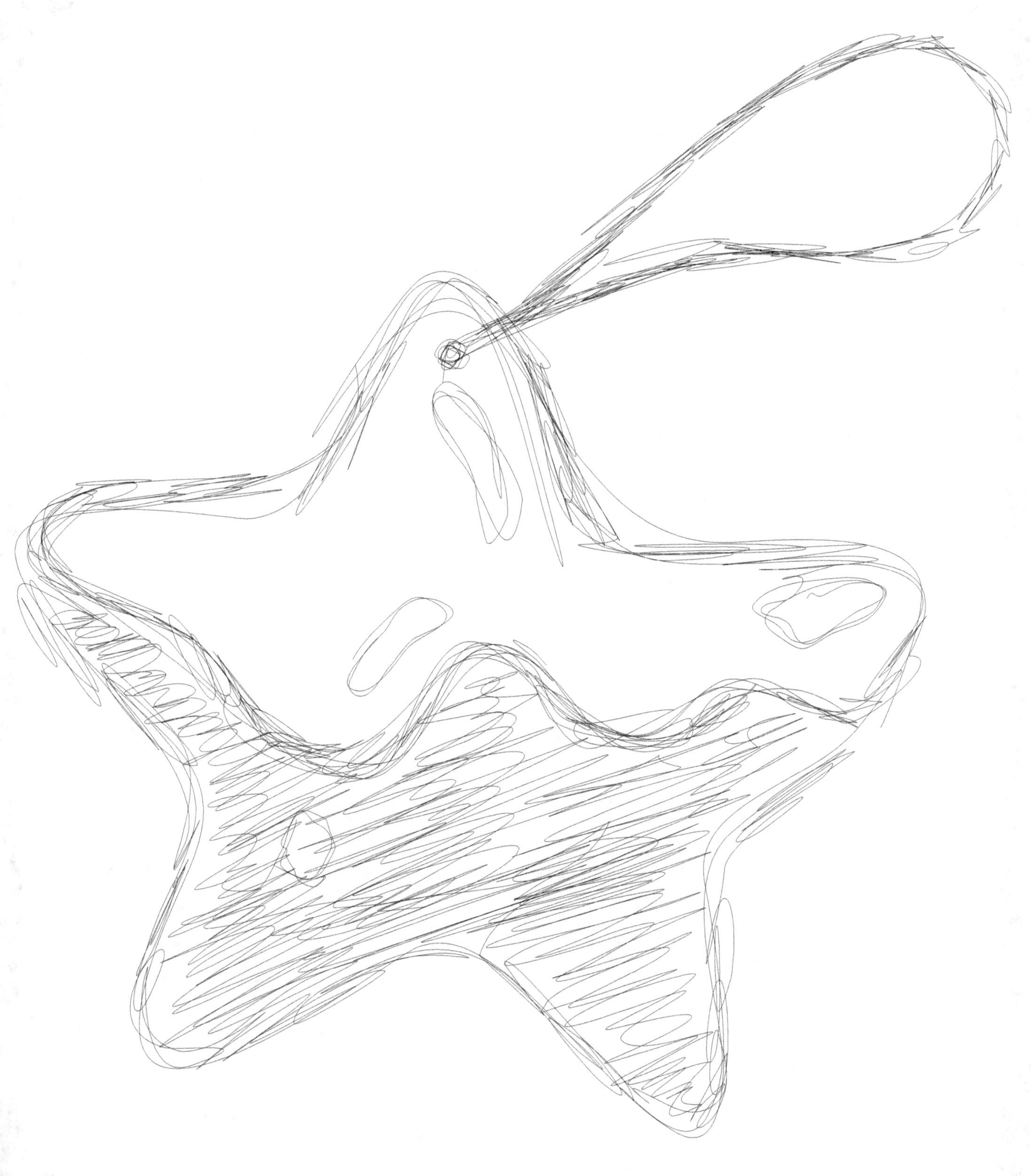

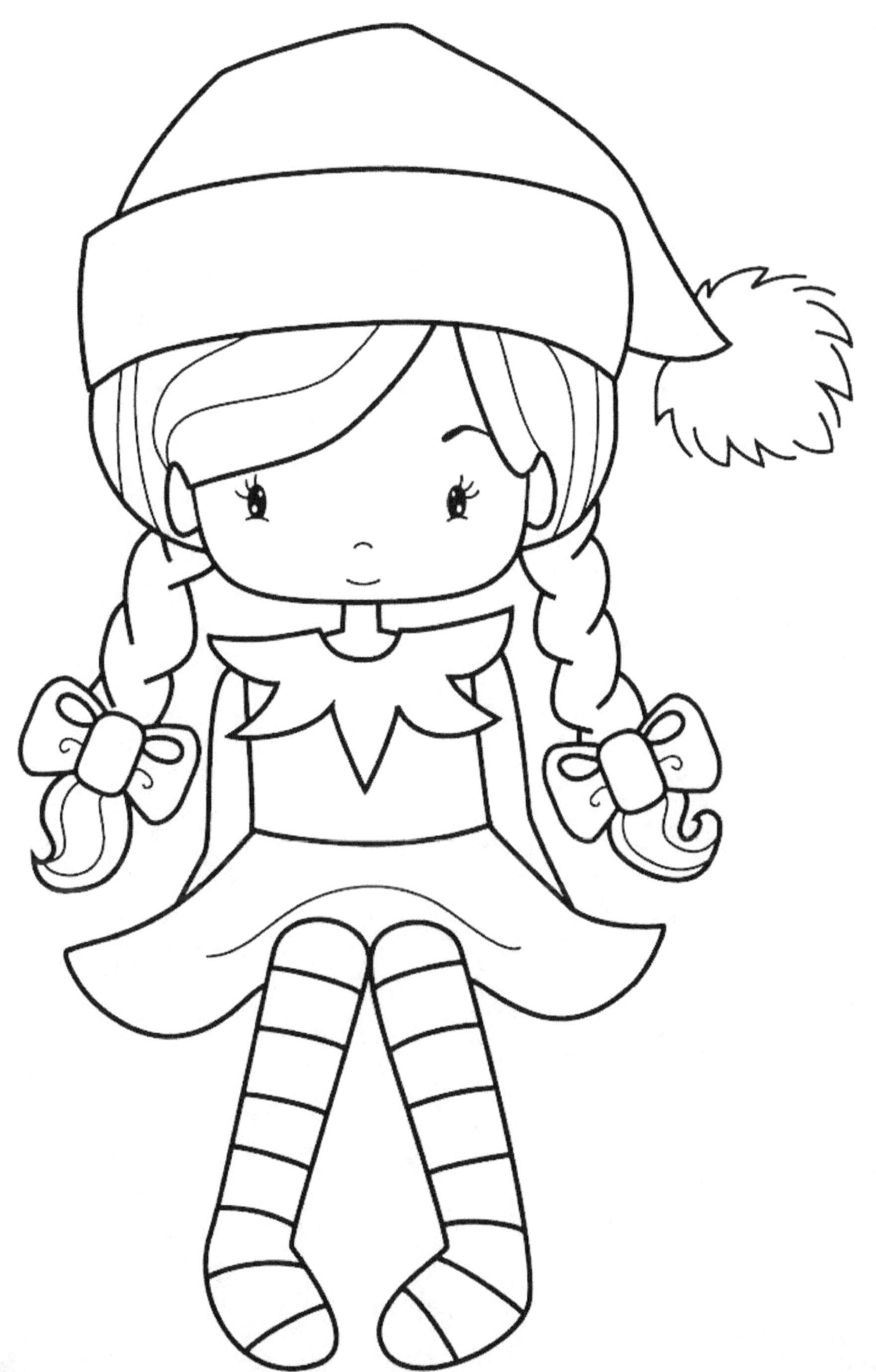

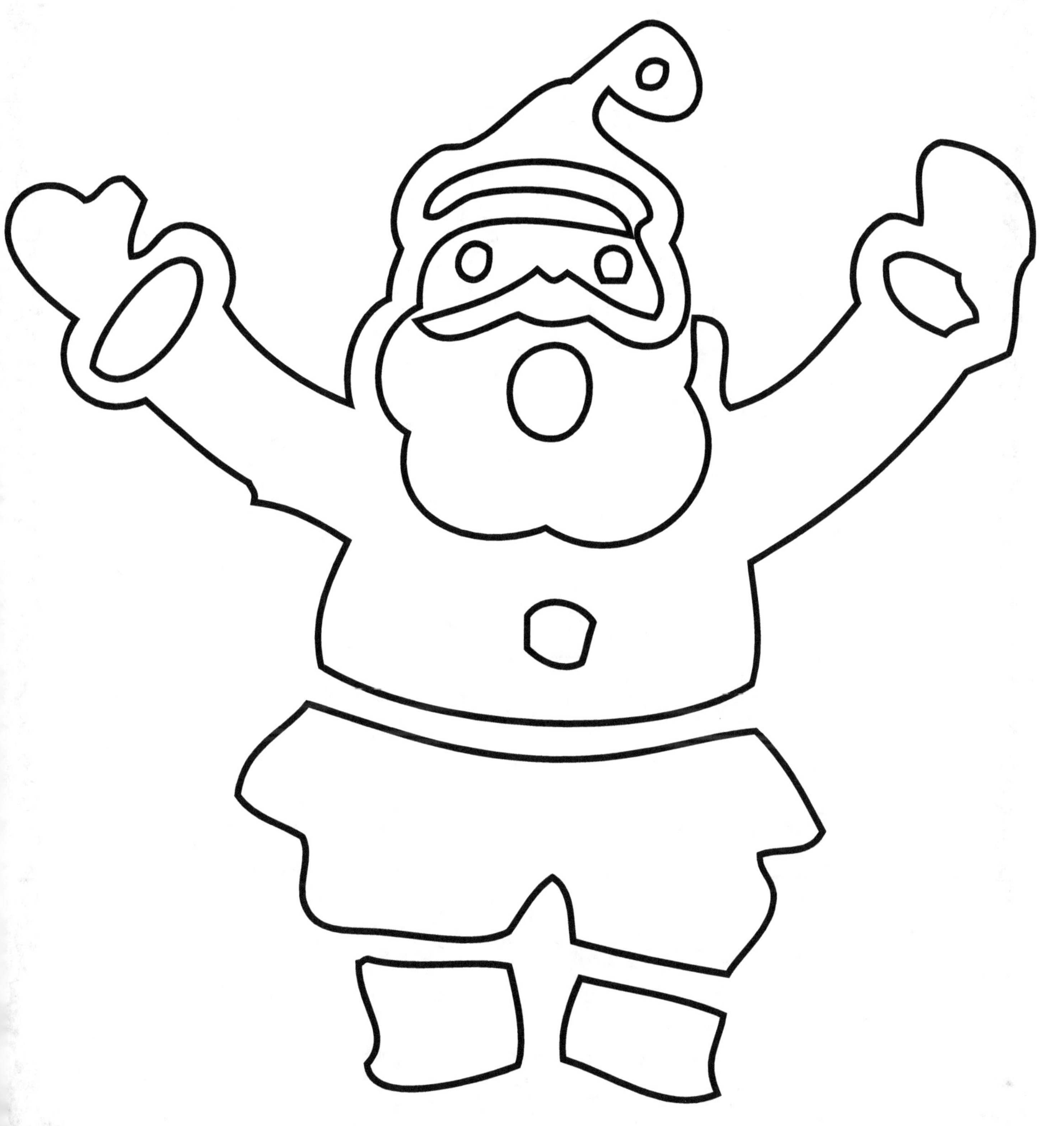

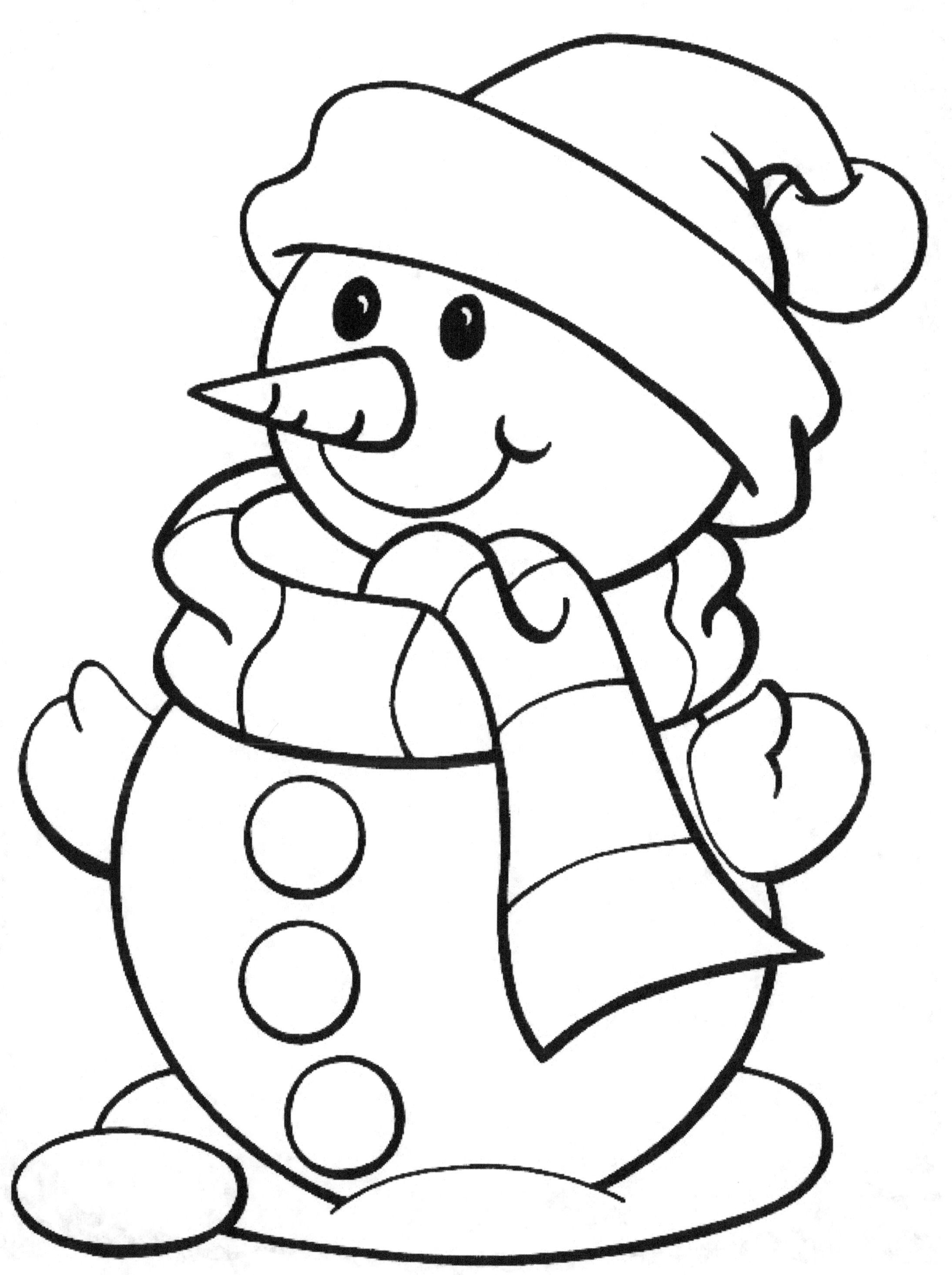

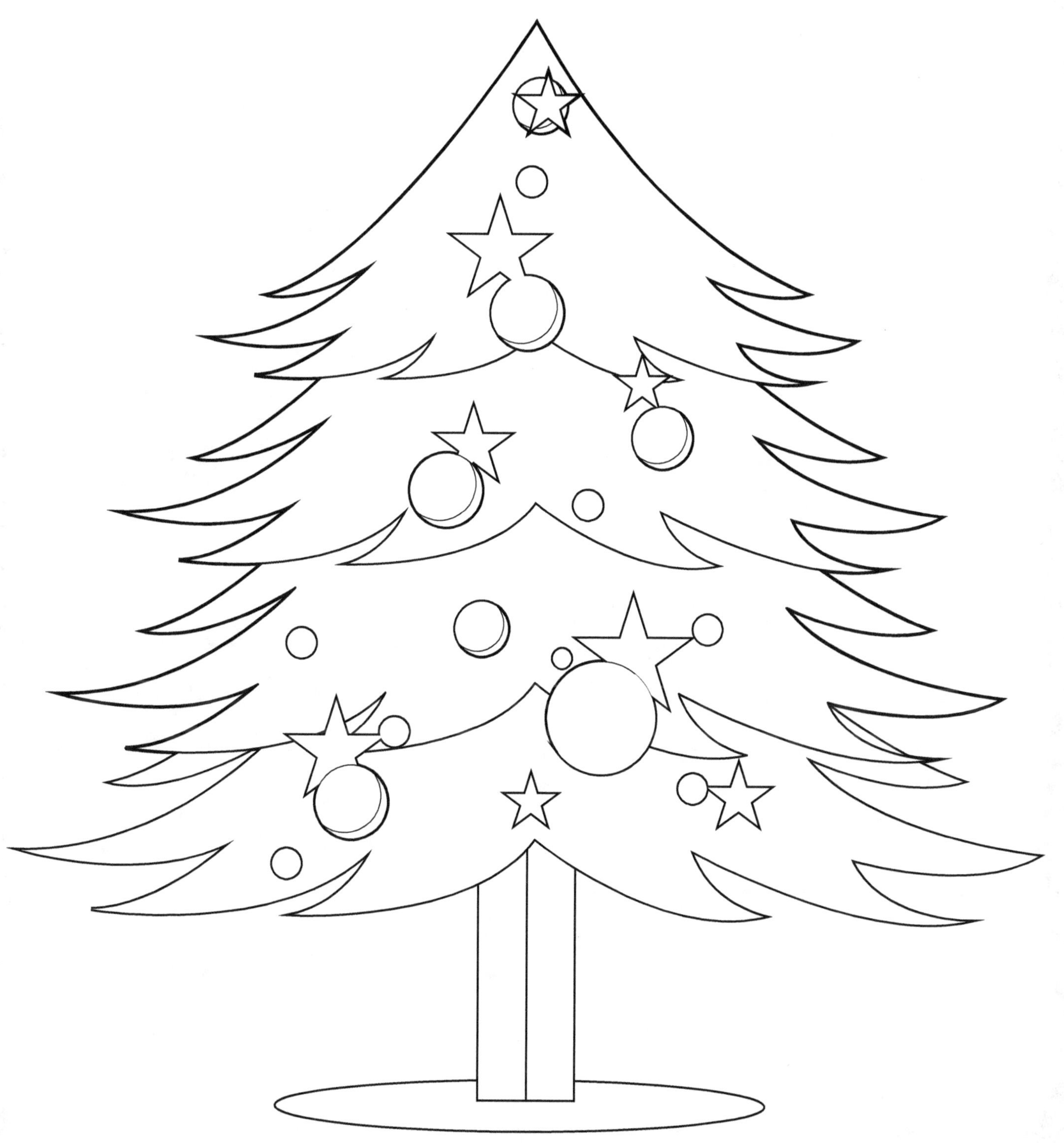

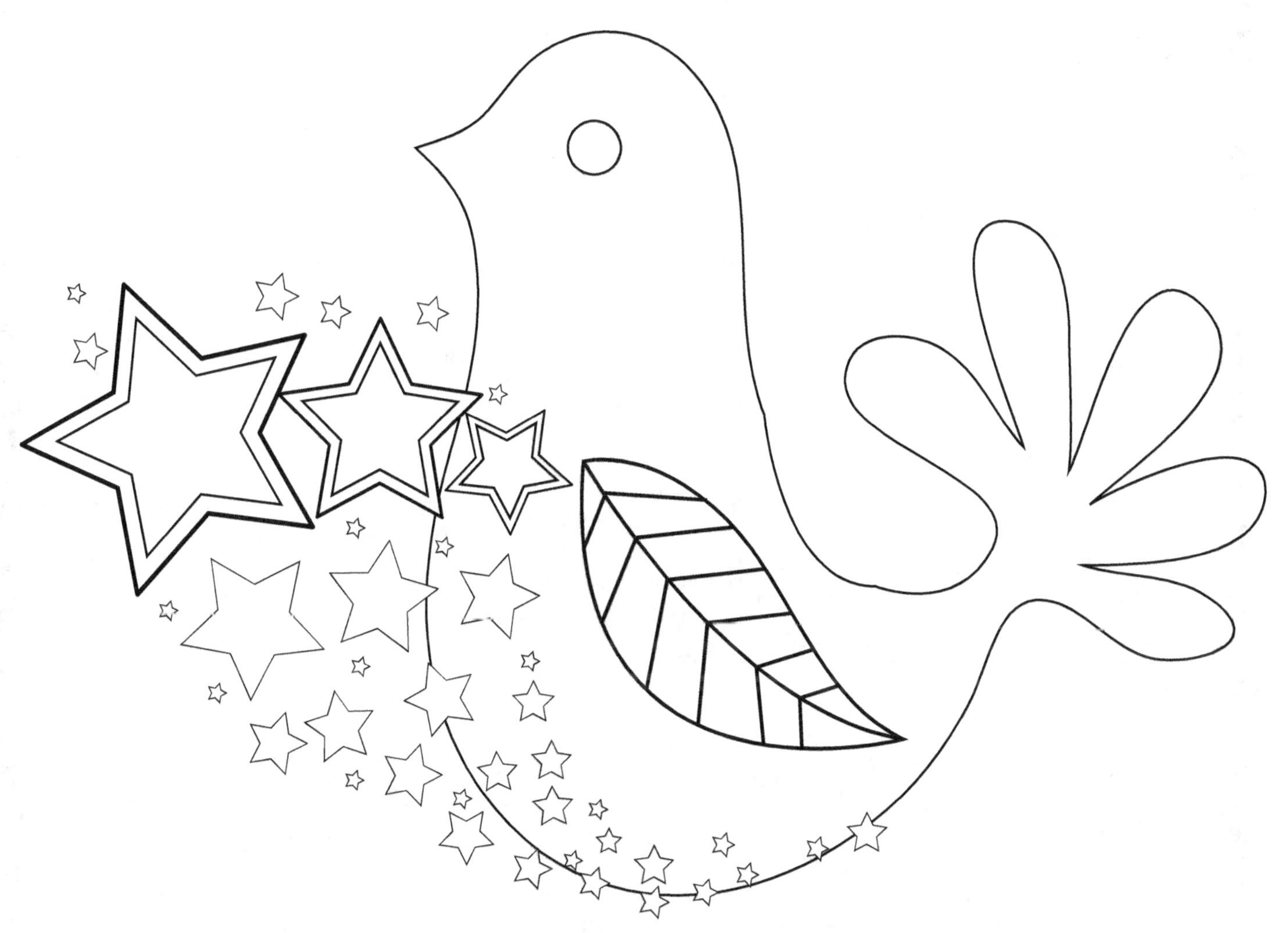

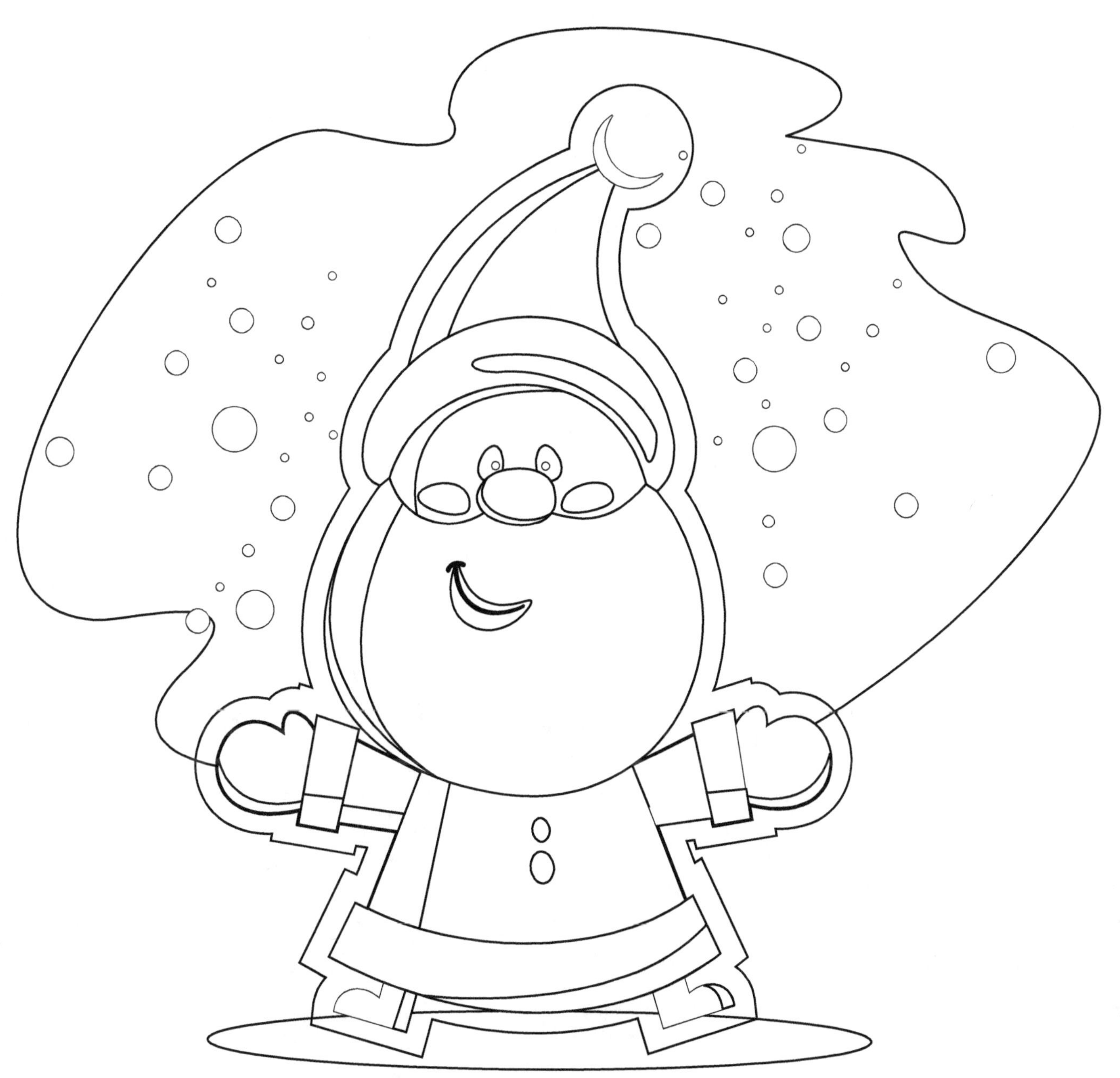

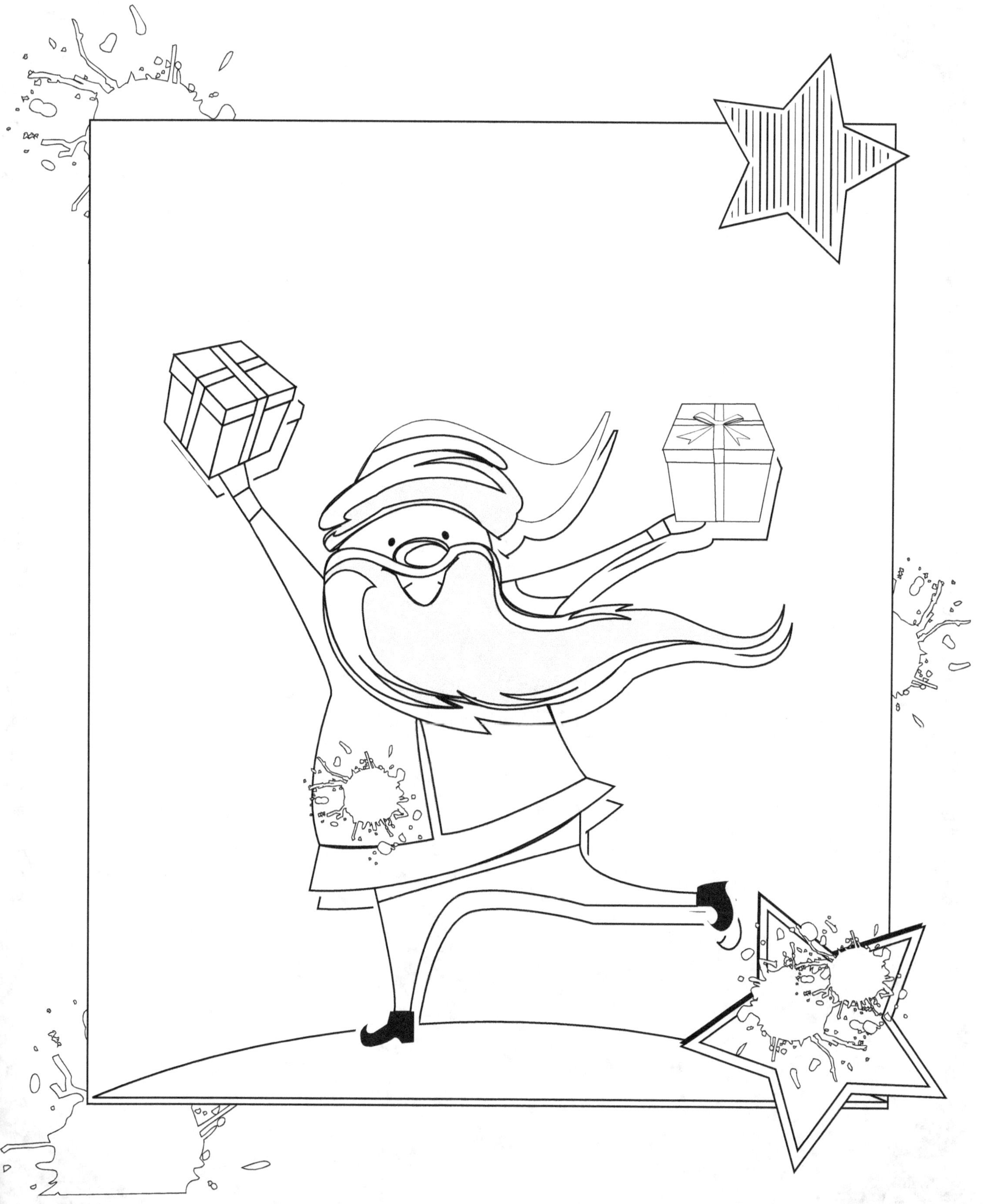

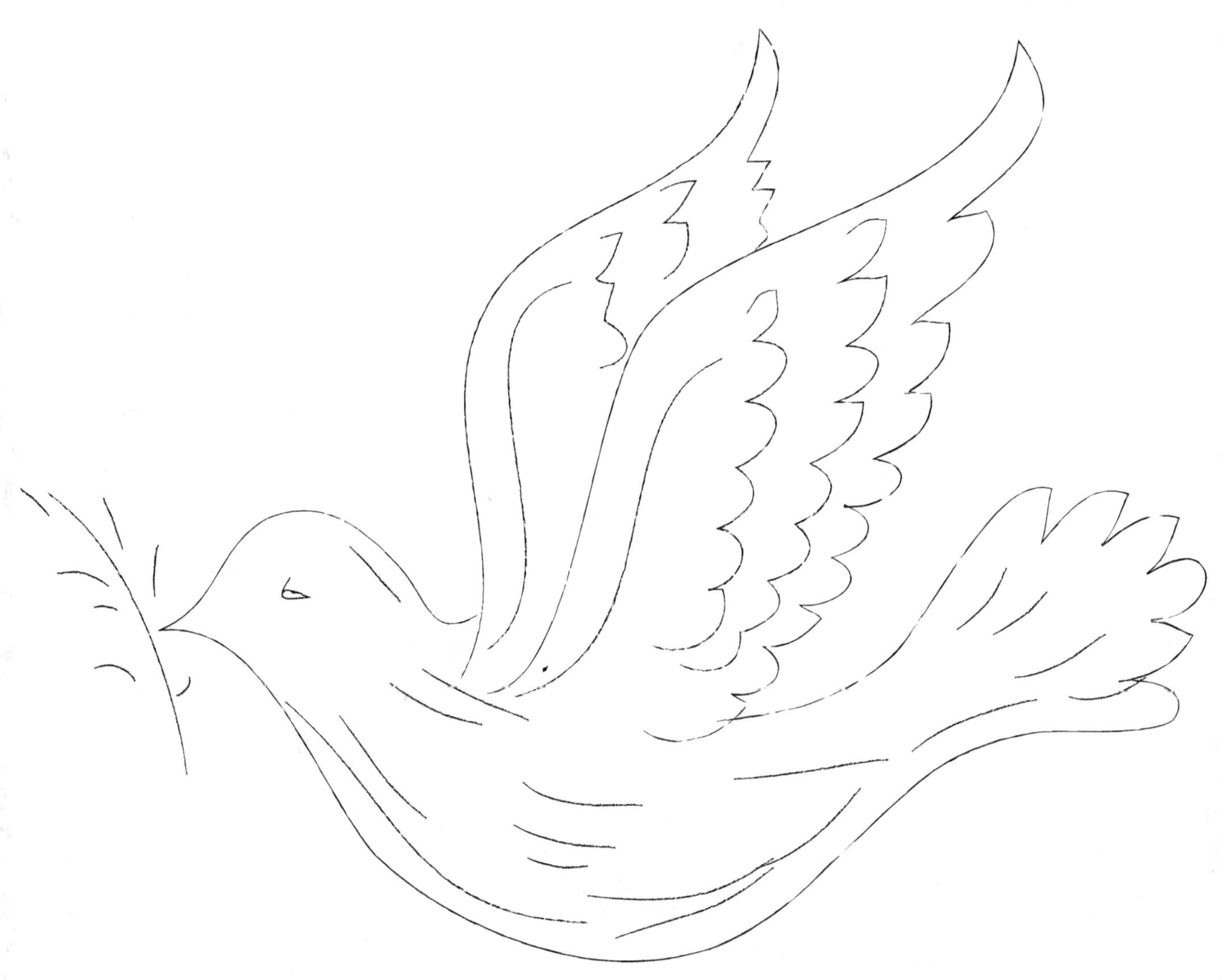

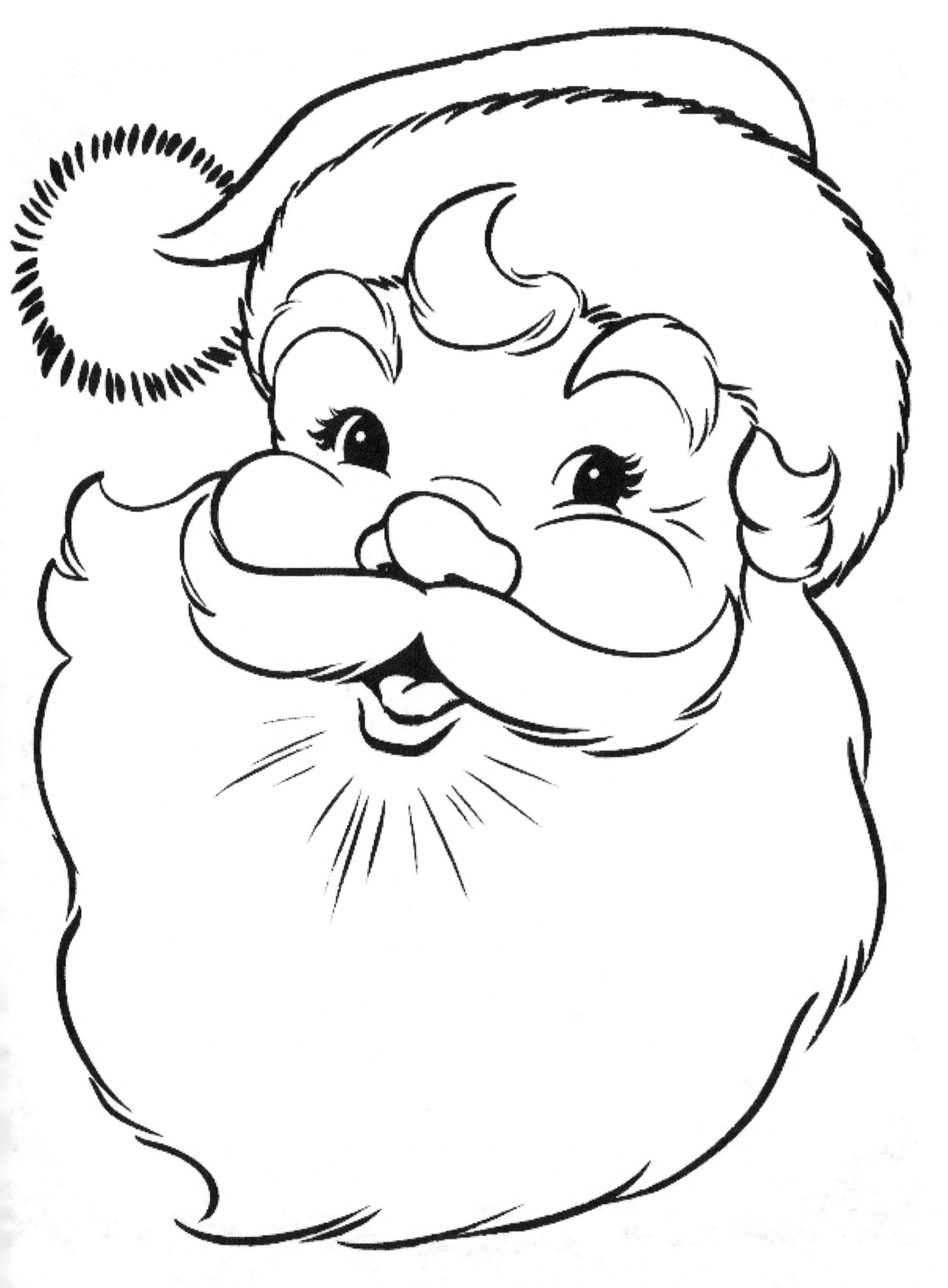

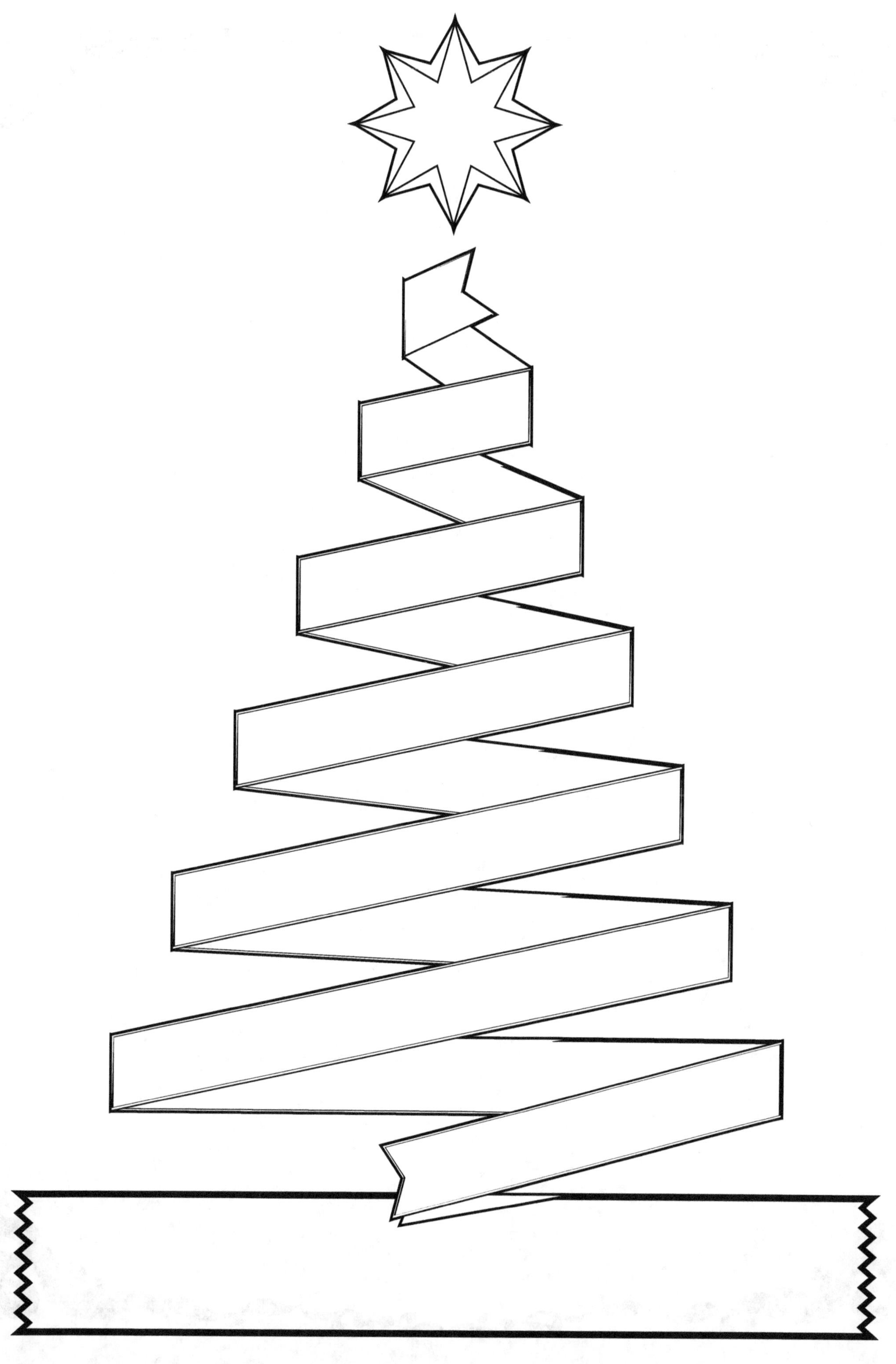

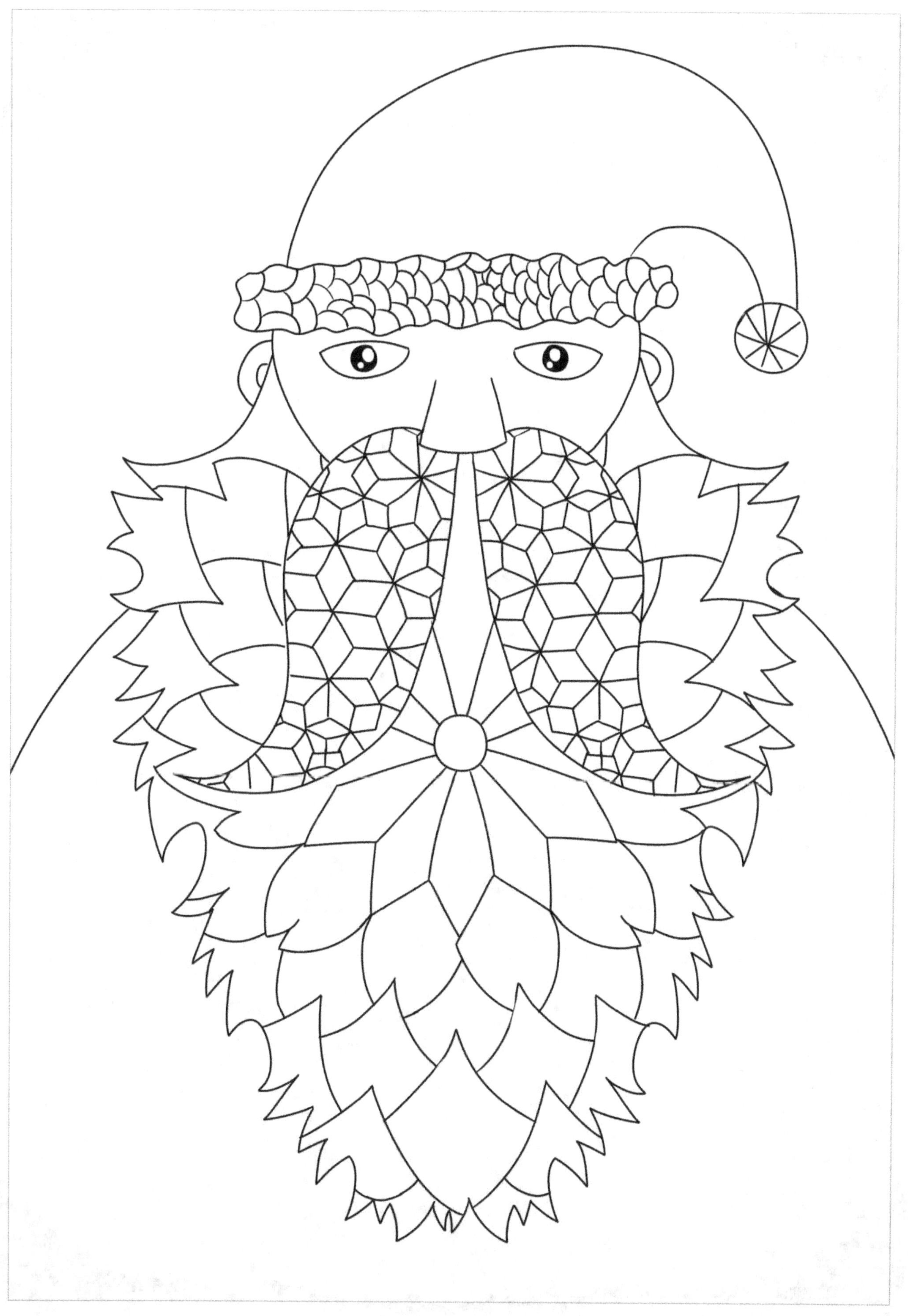

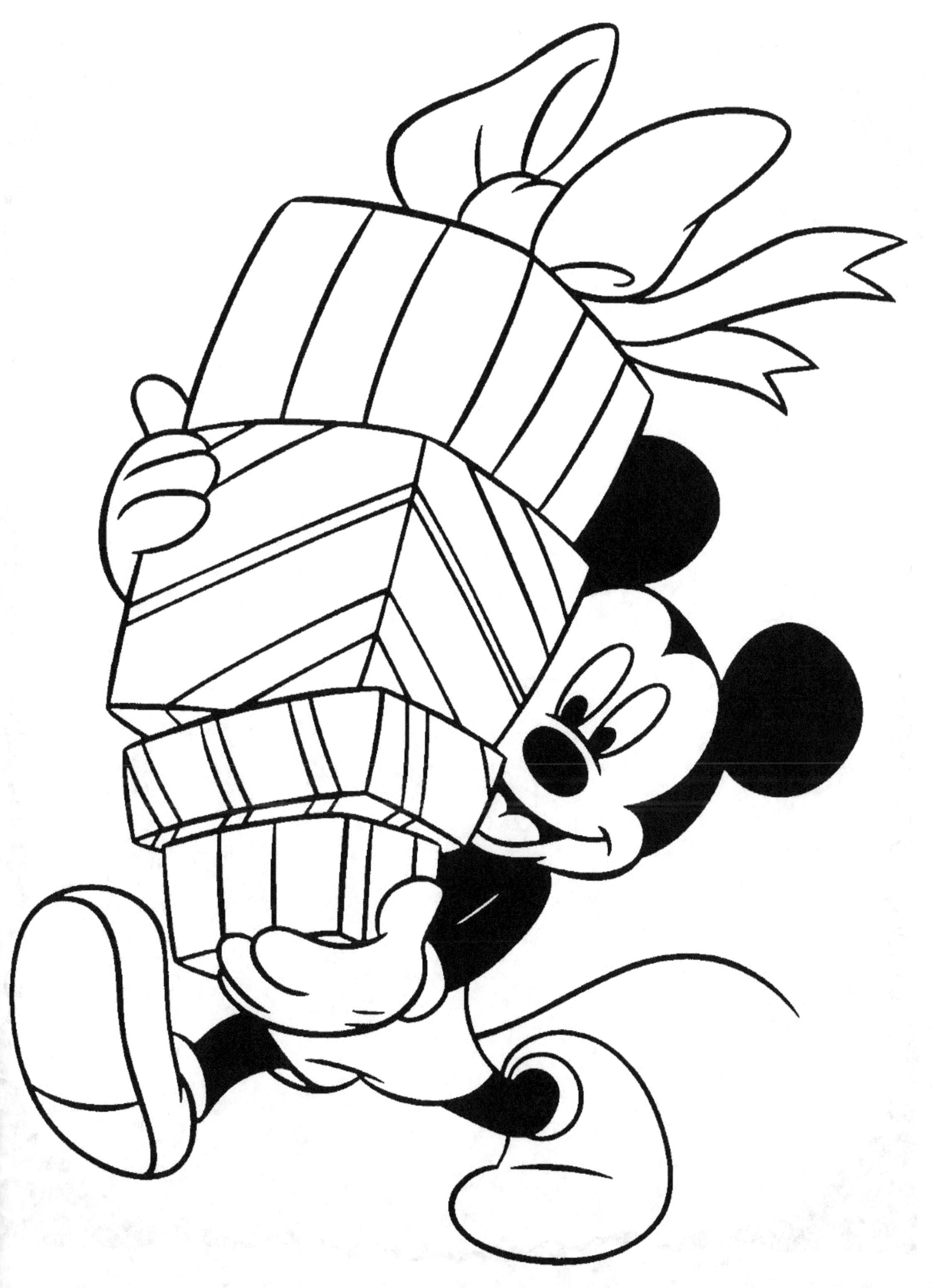

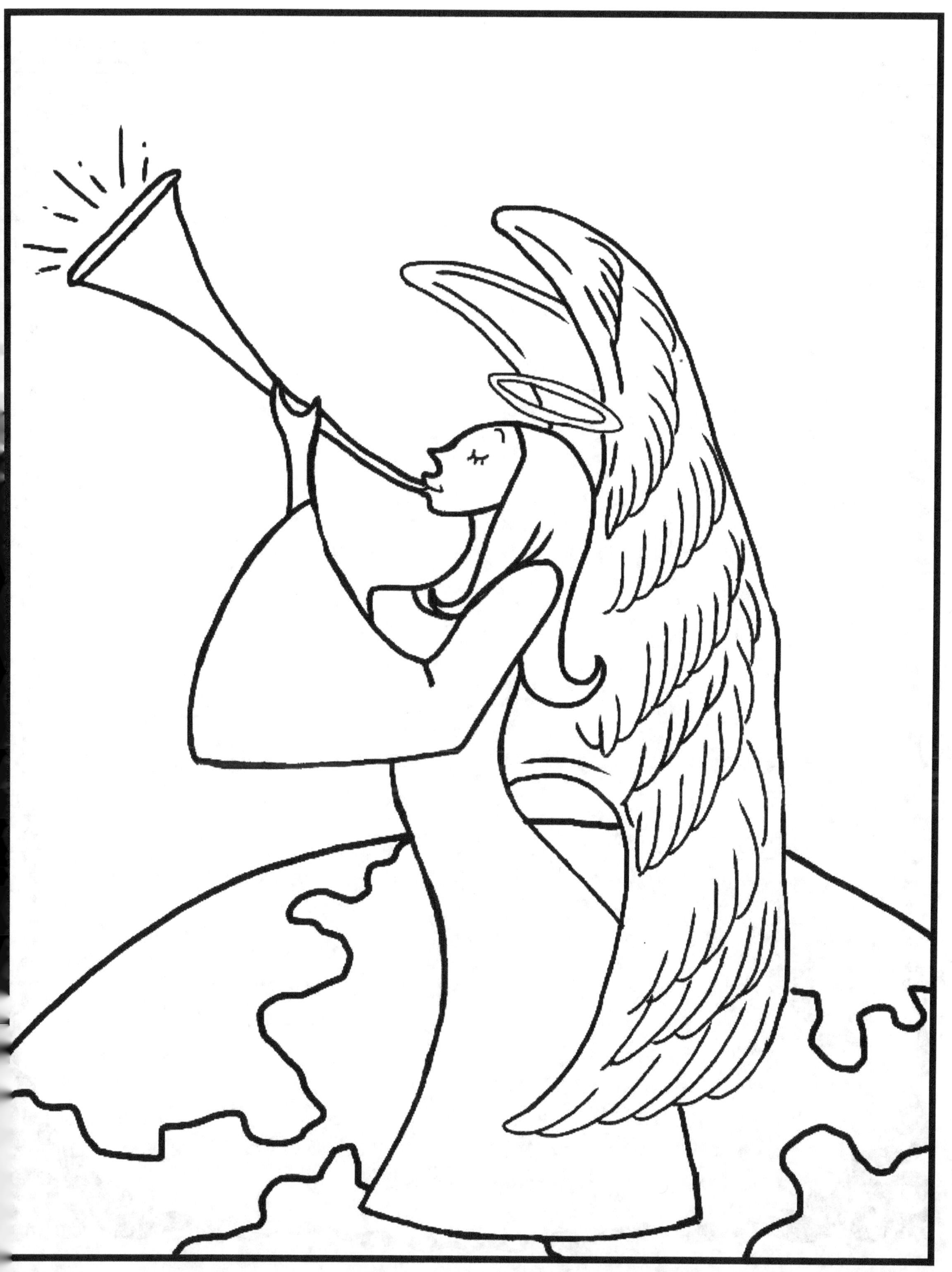

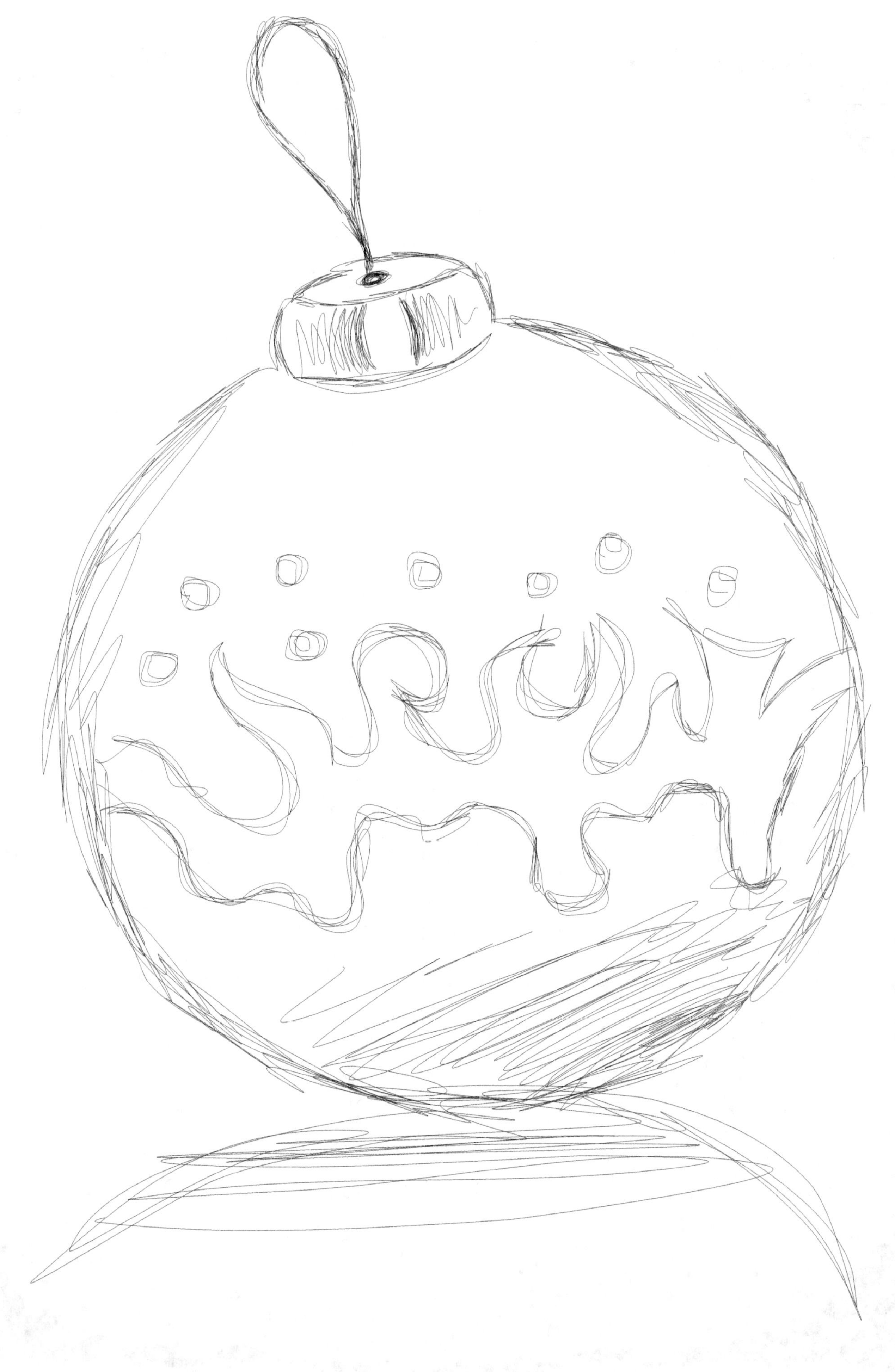

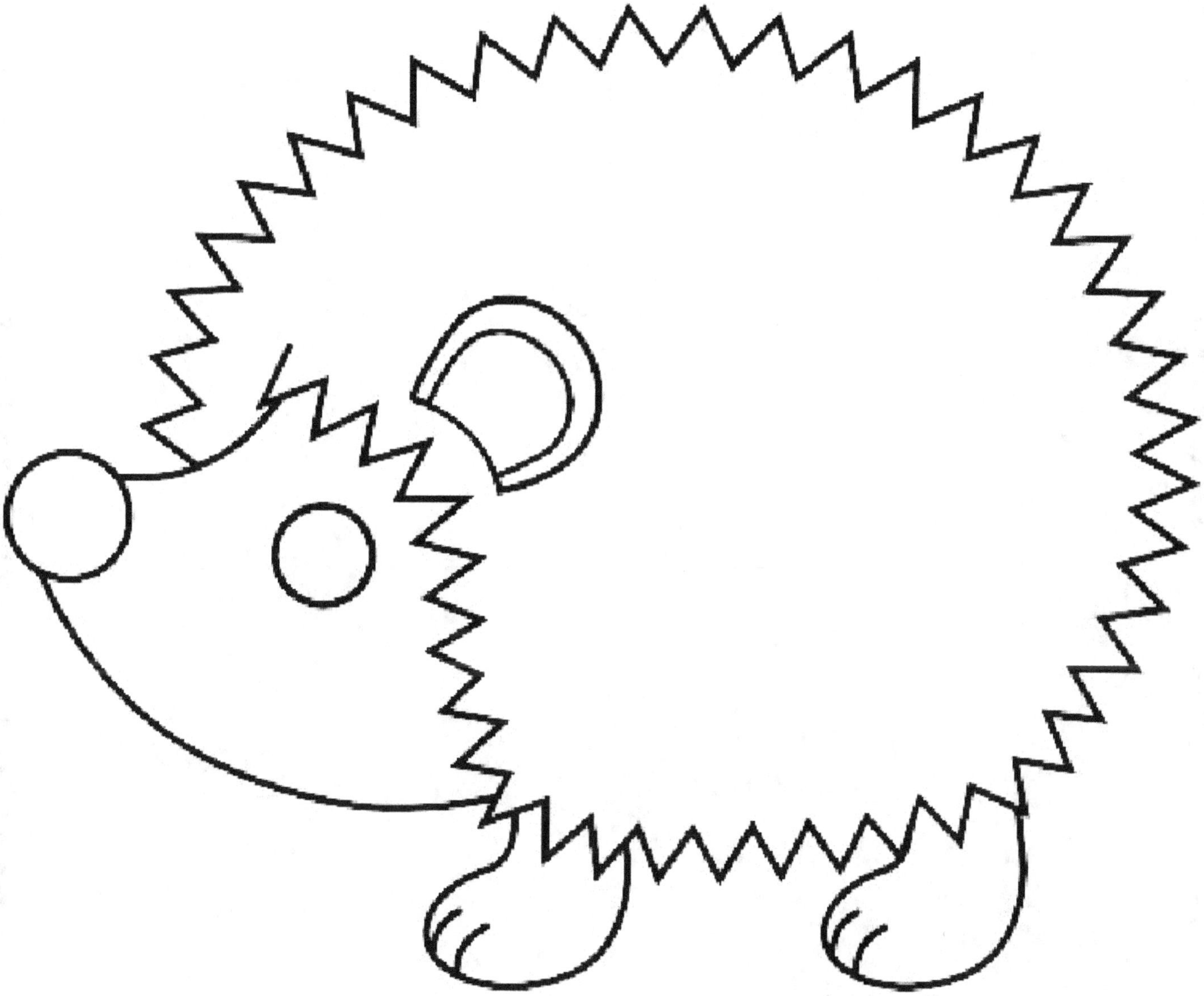

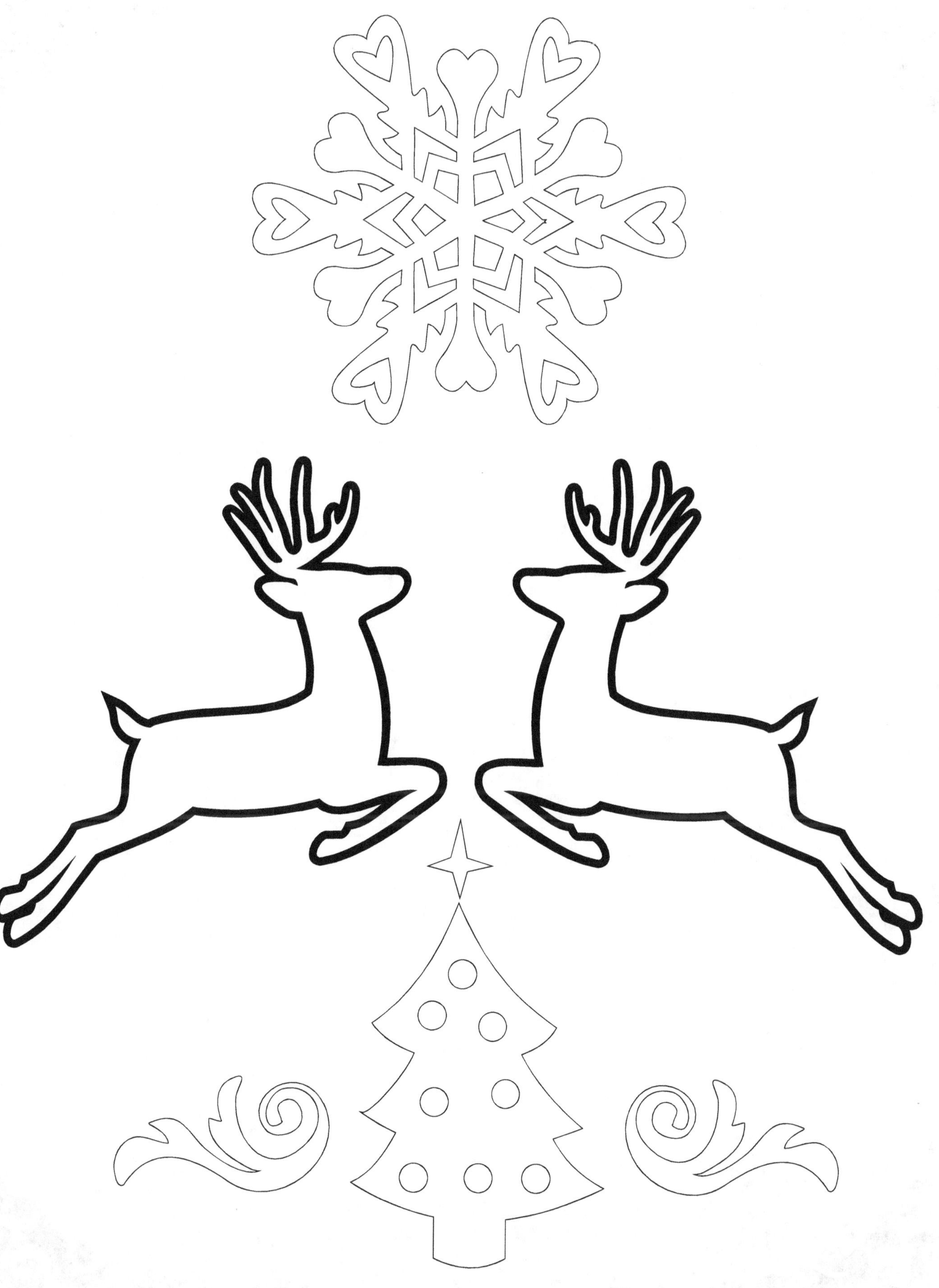

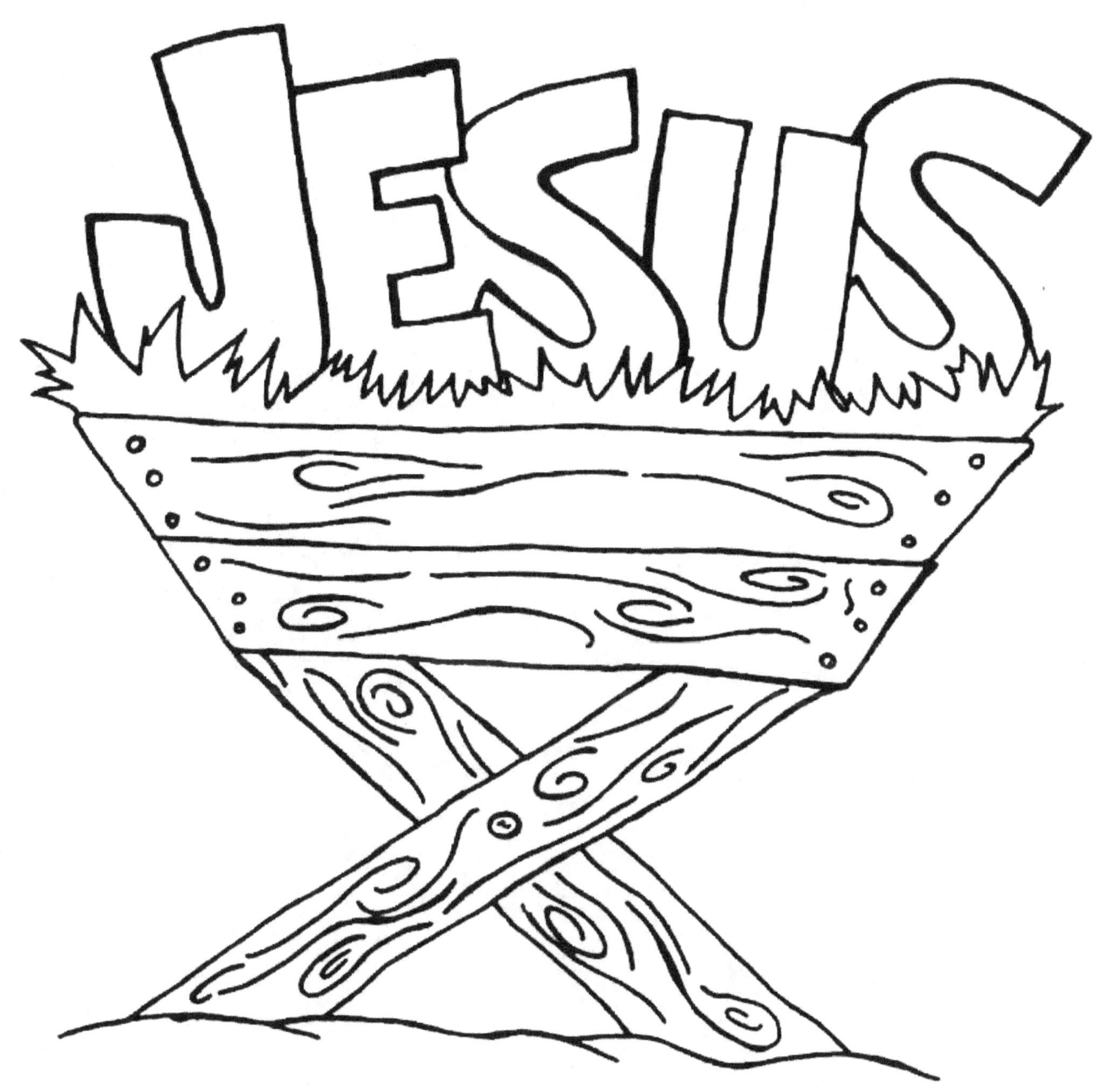

JESUS

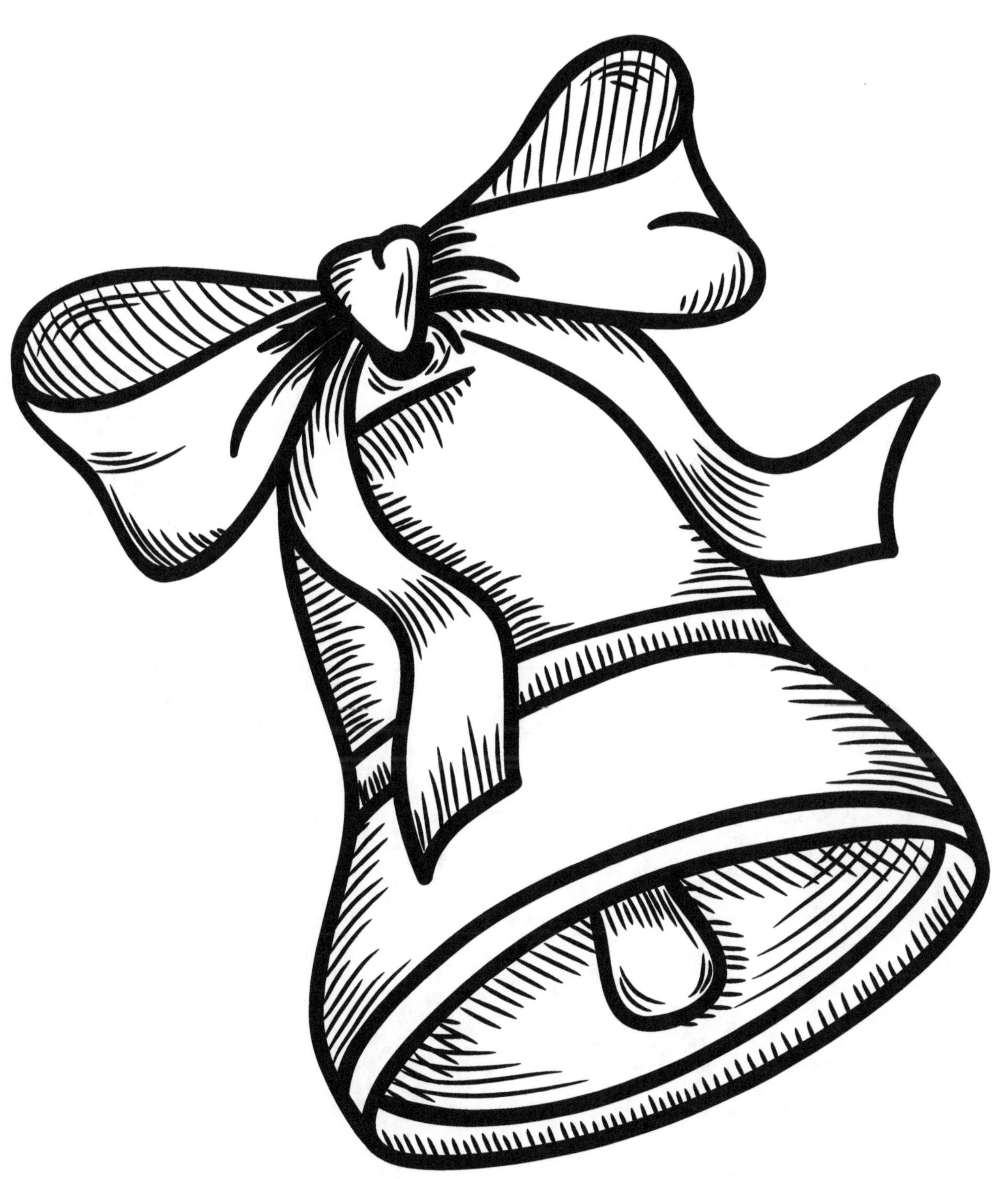

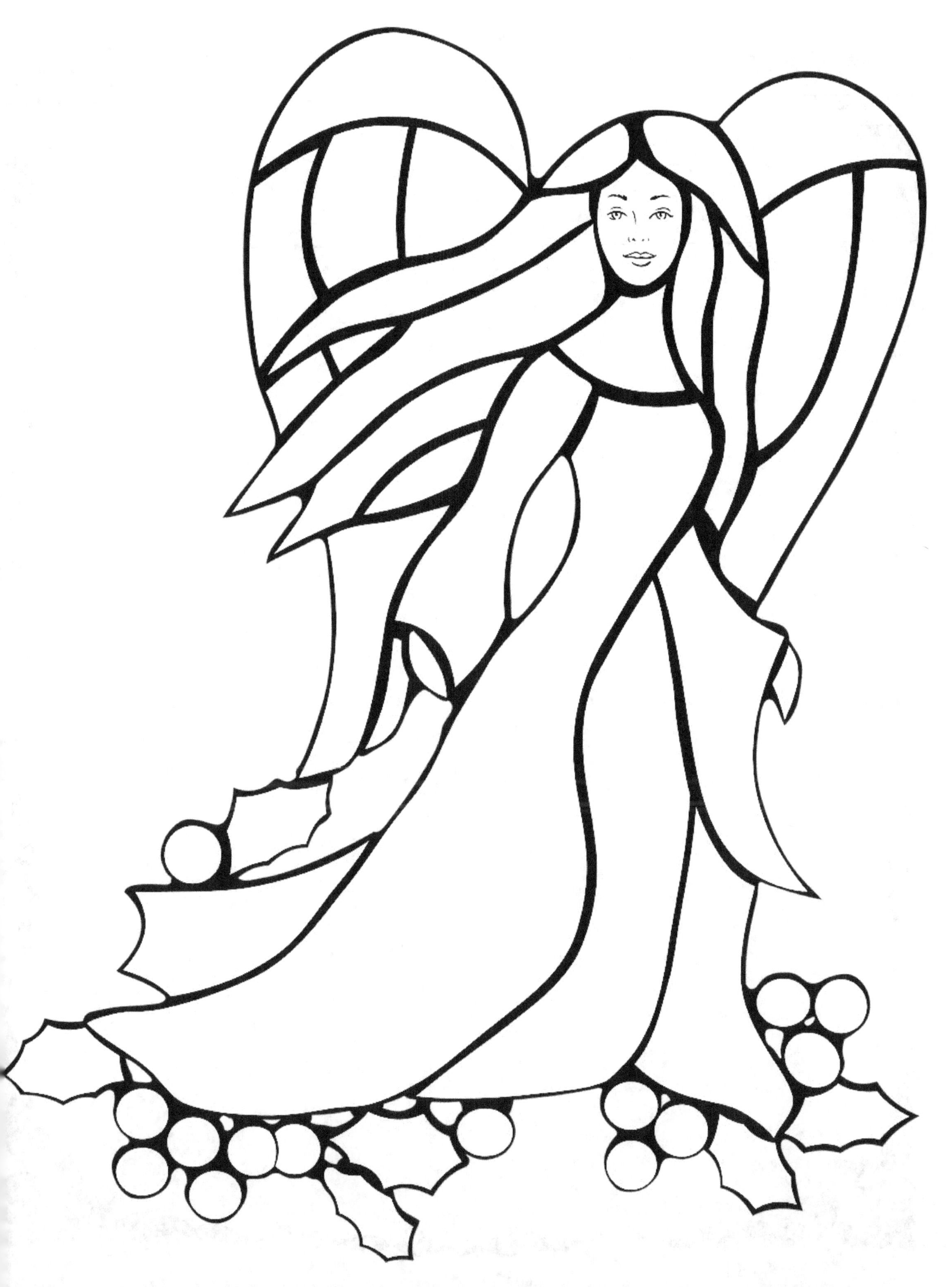

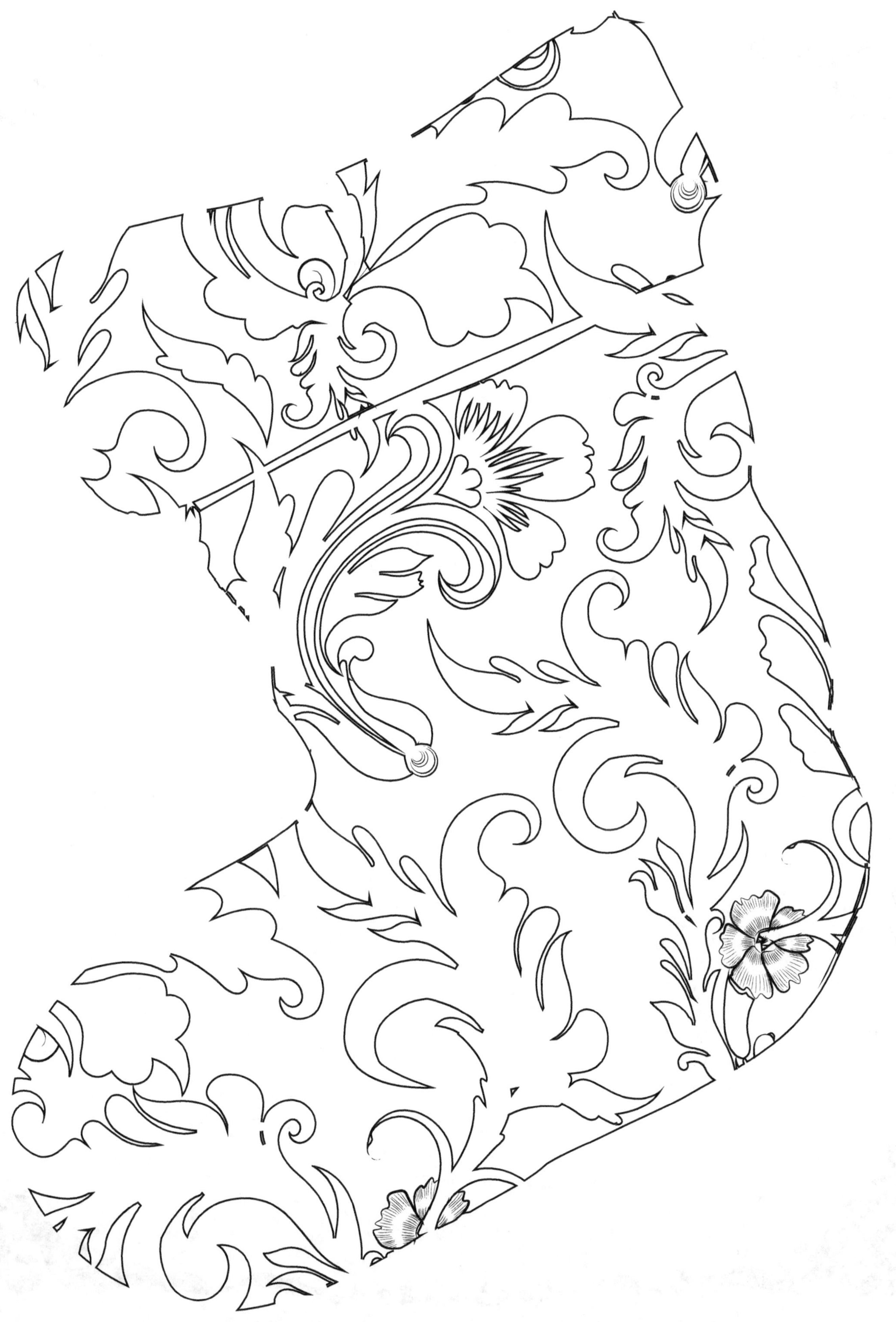

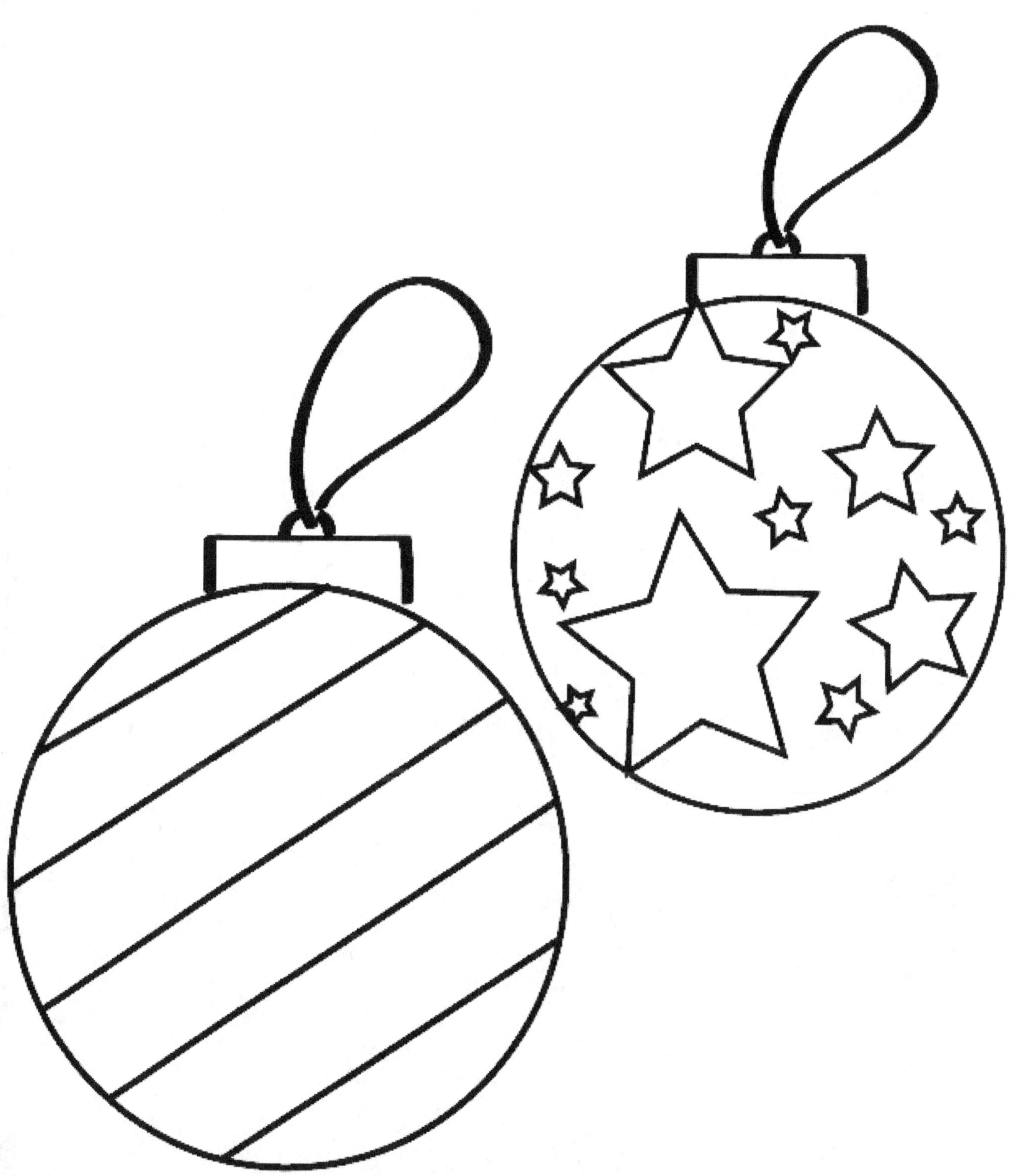

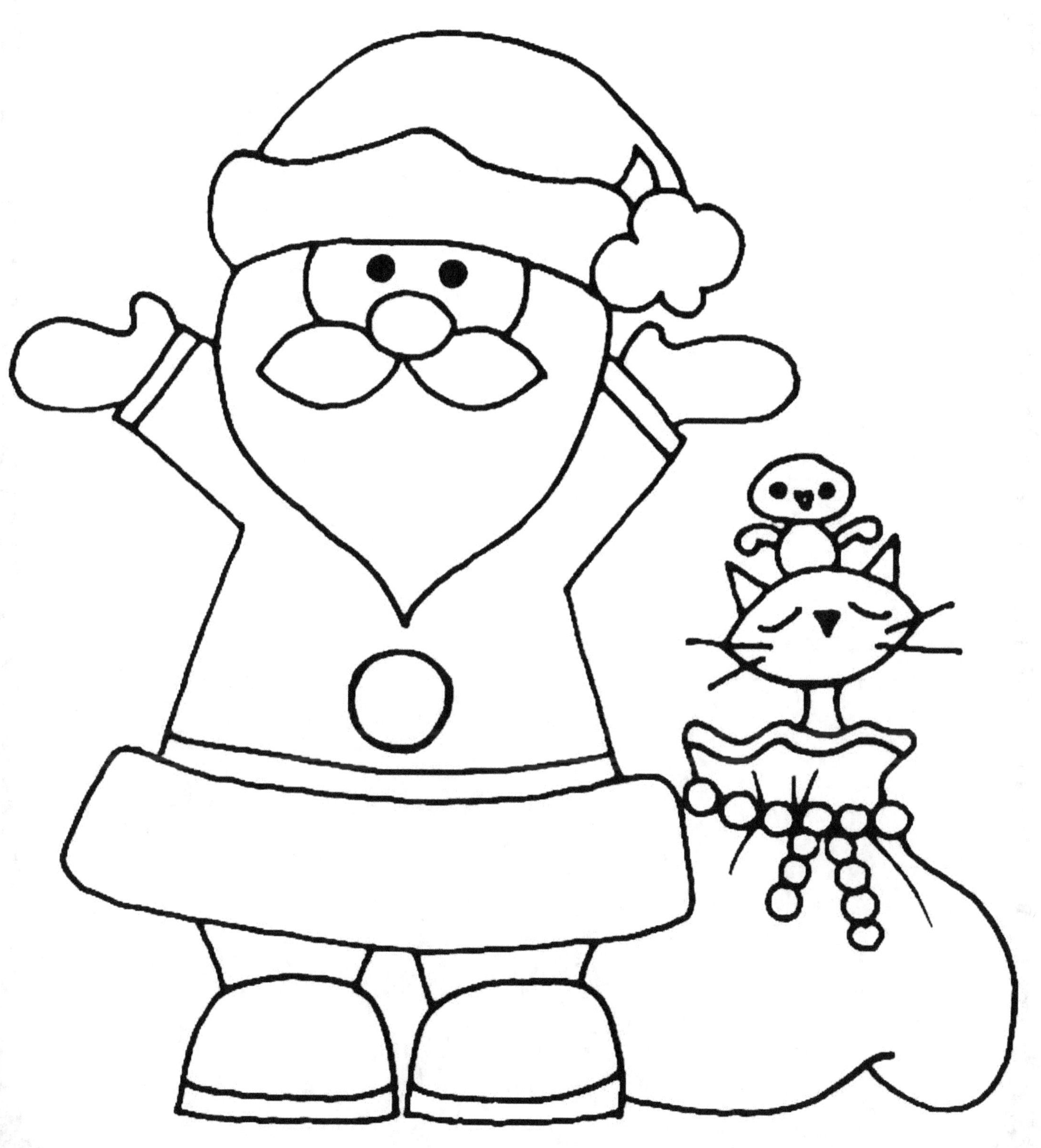

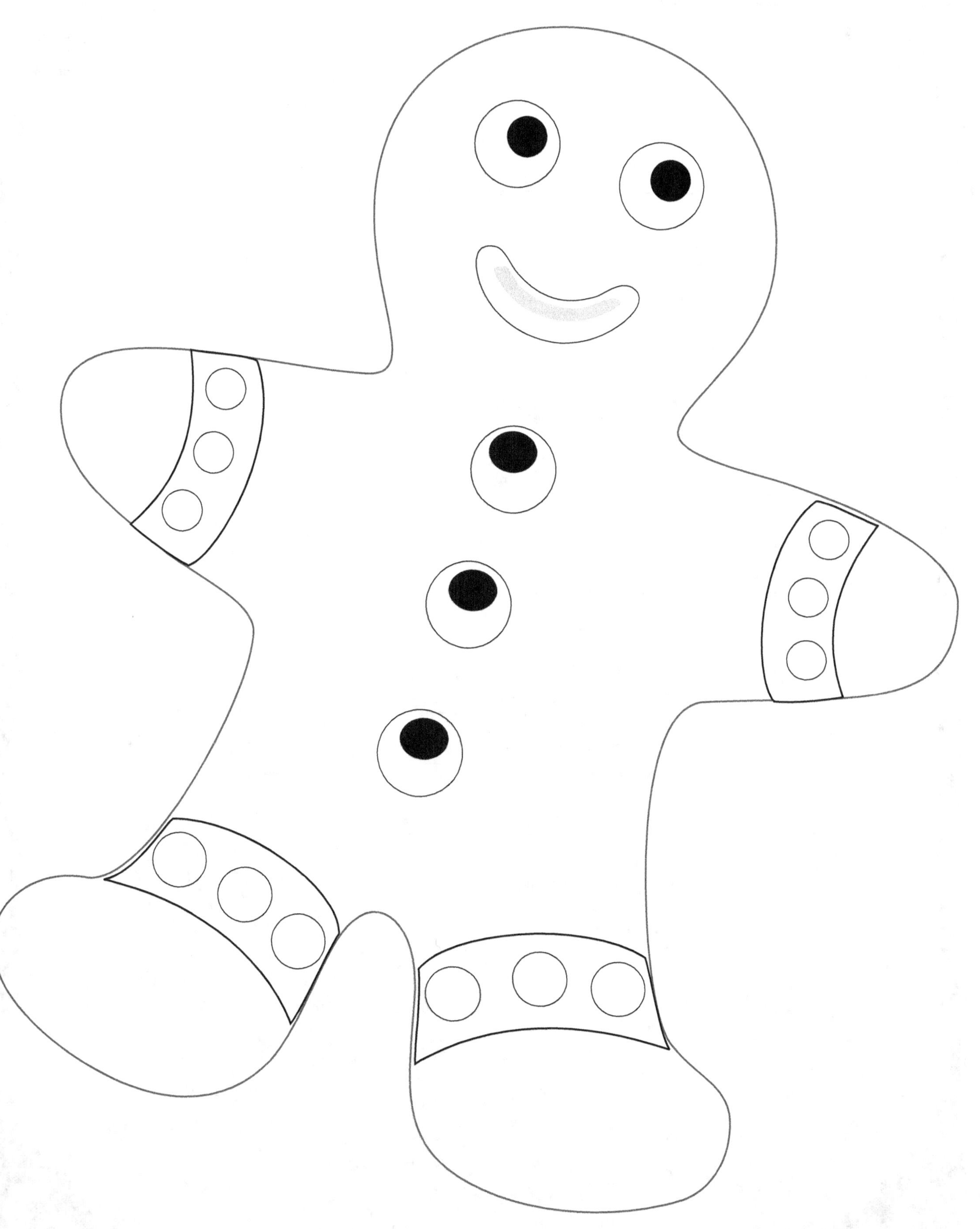

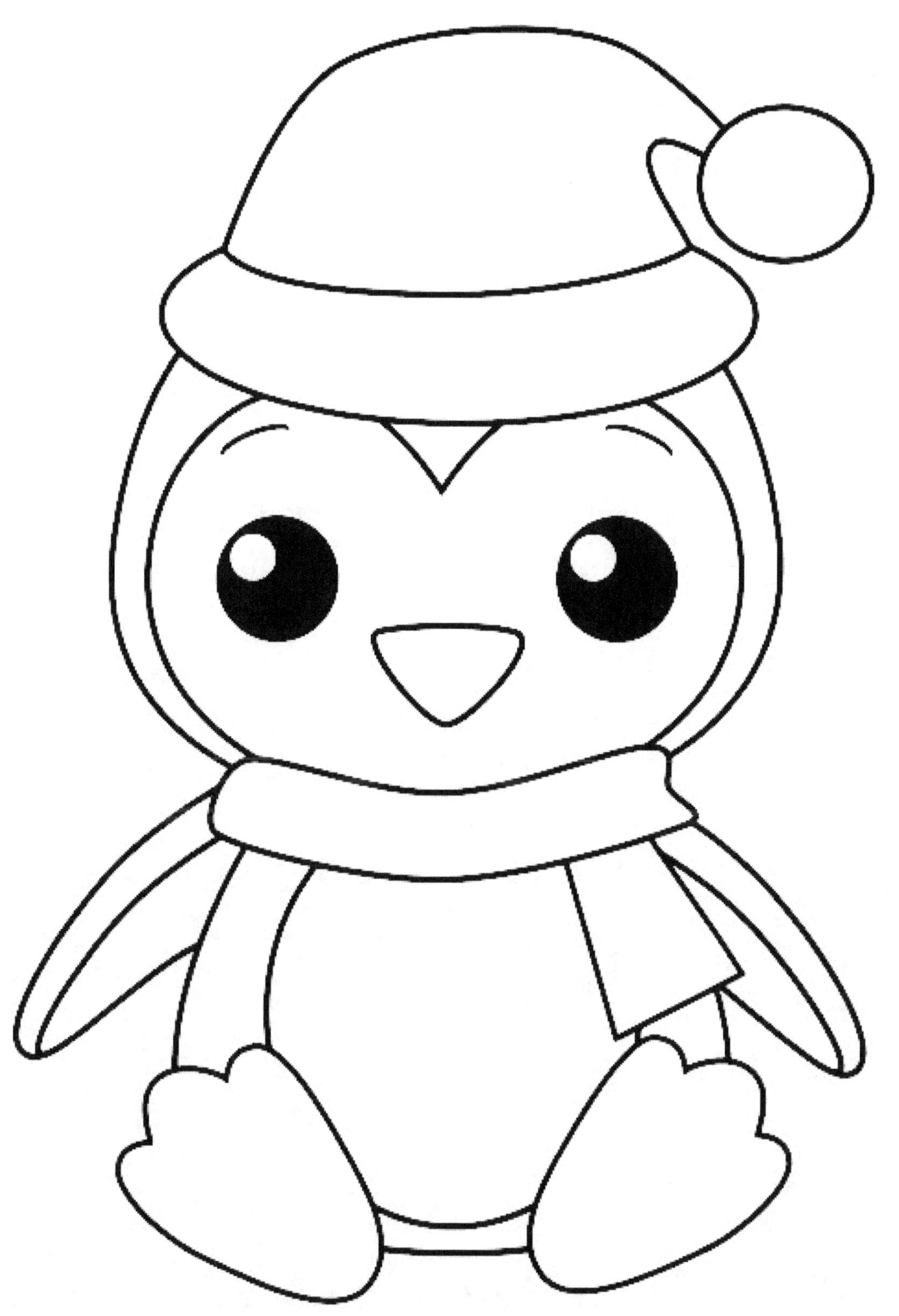

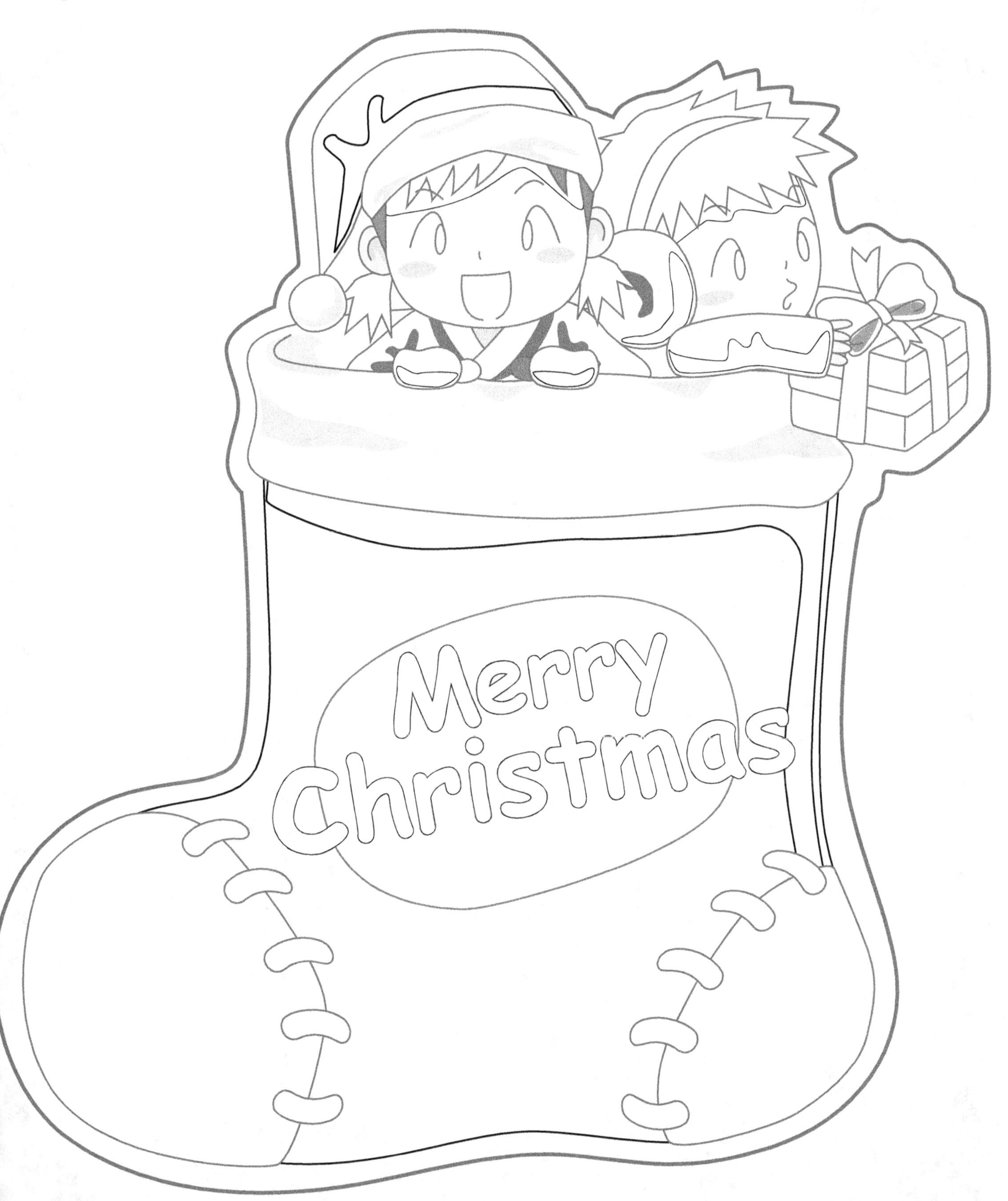
Merry
Christmas

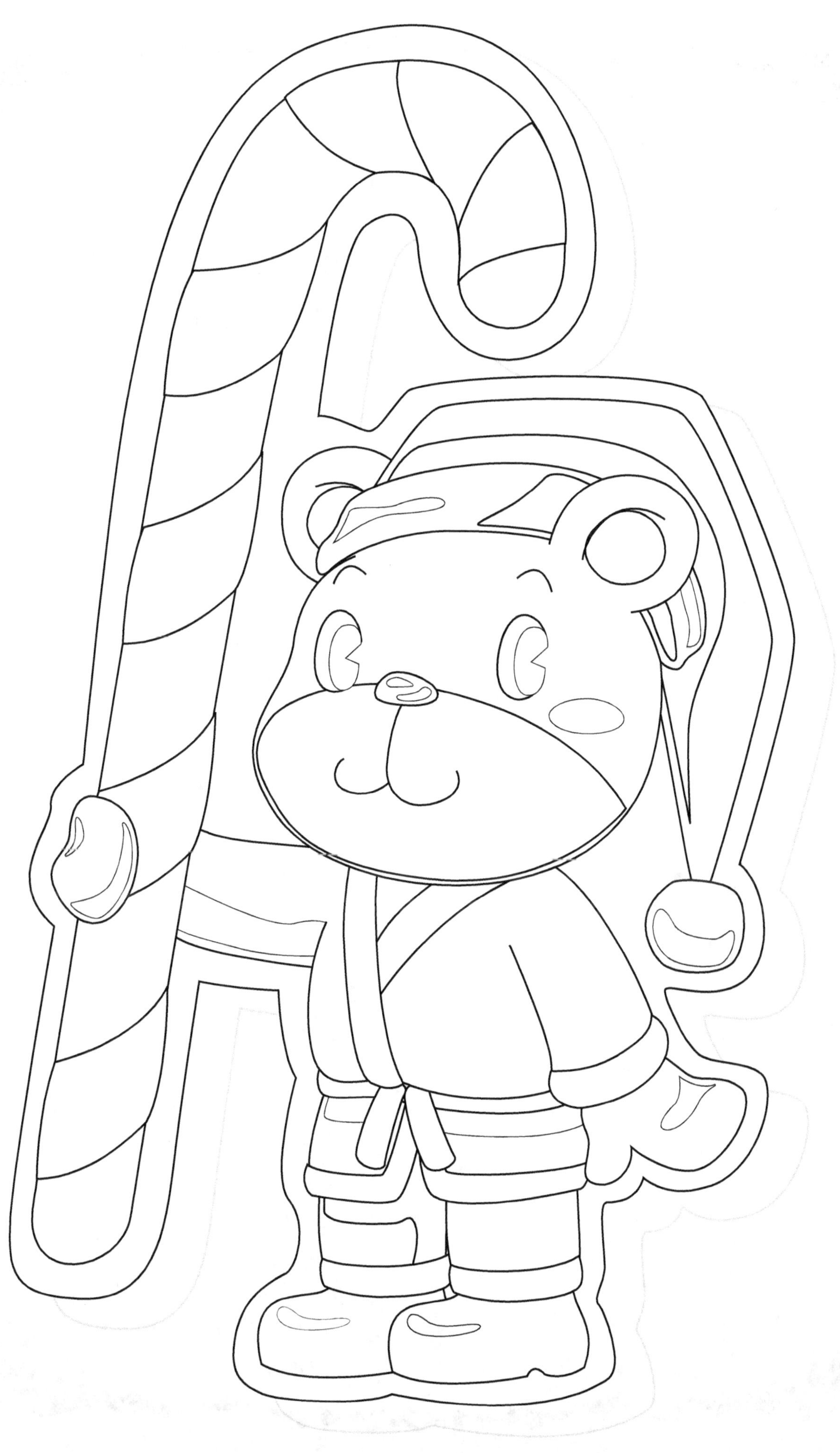

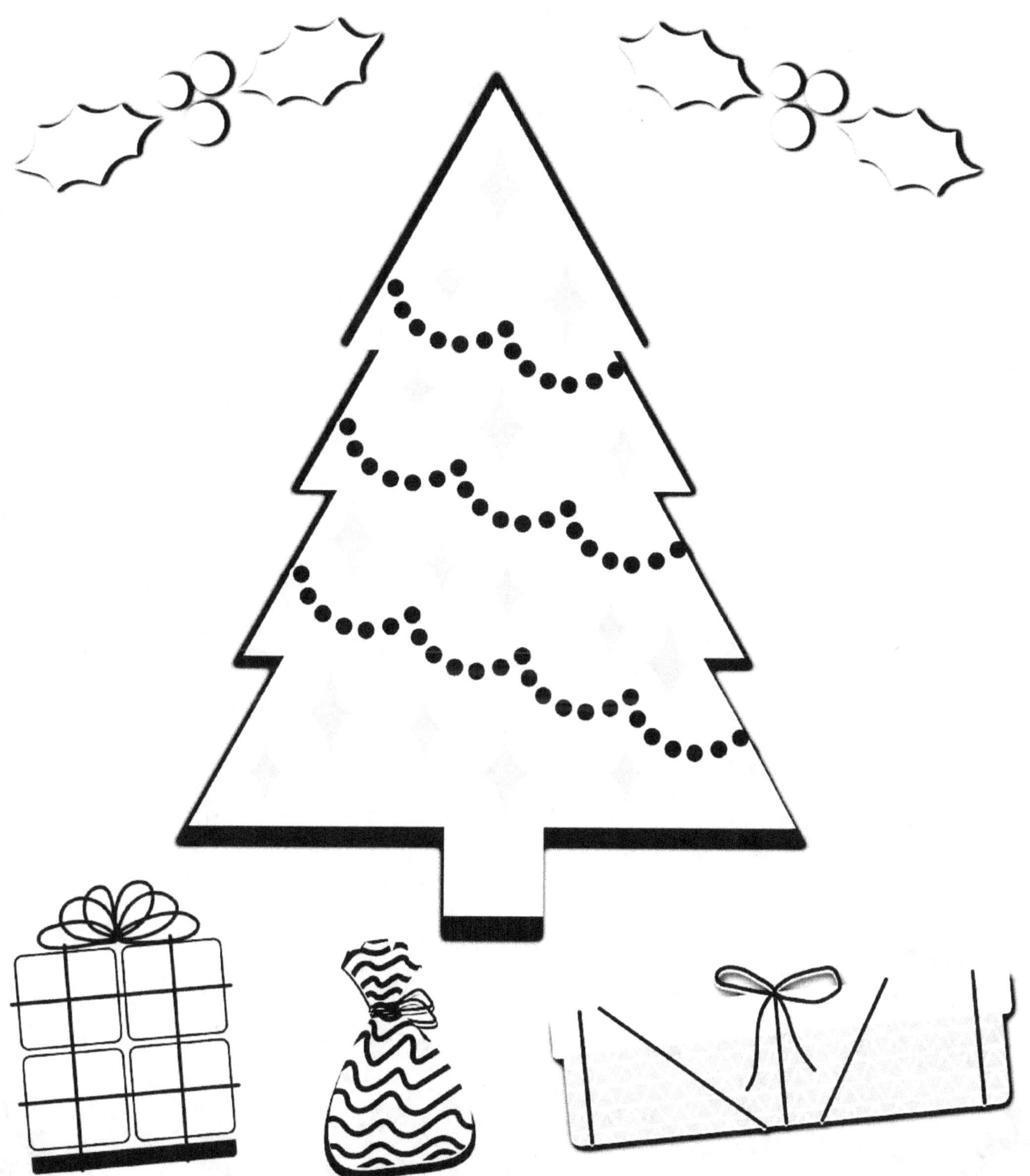

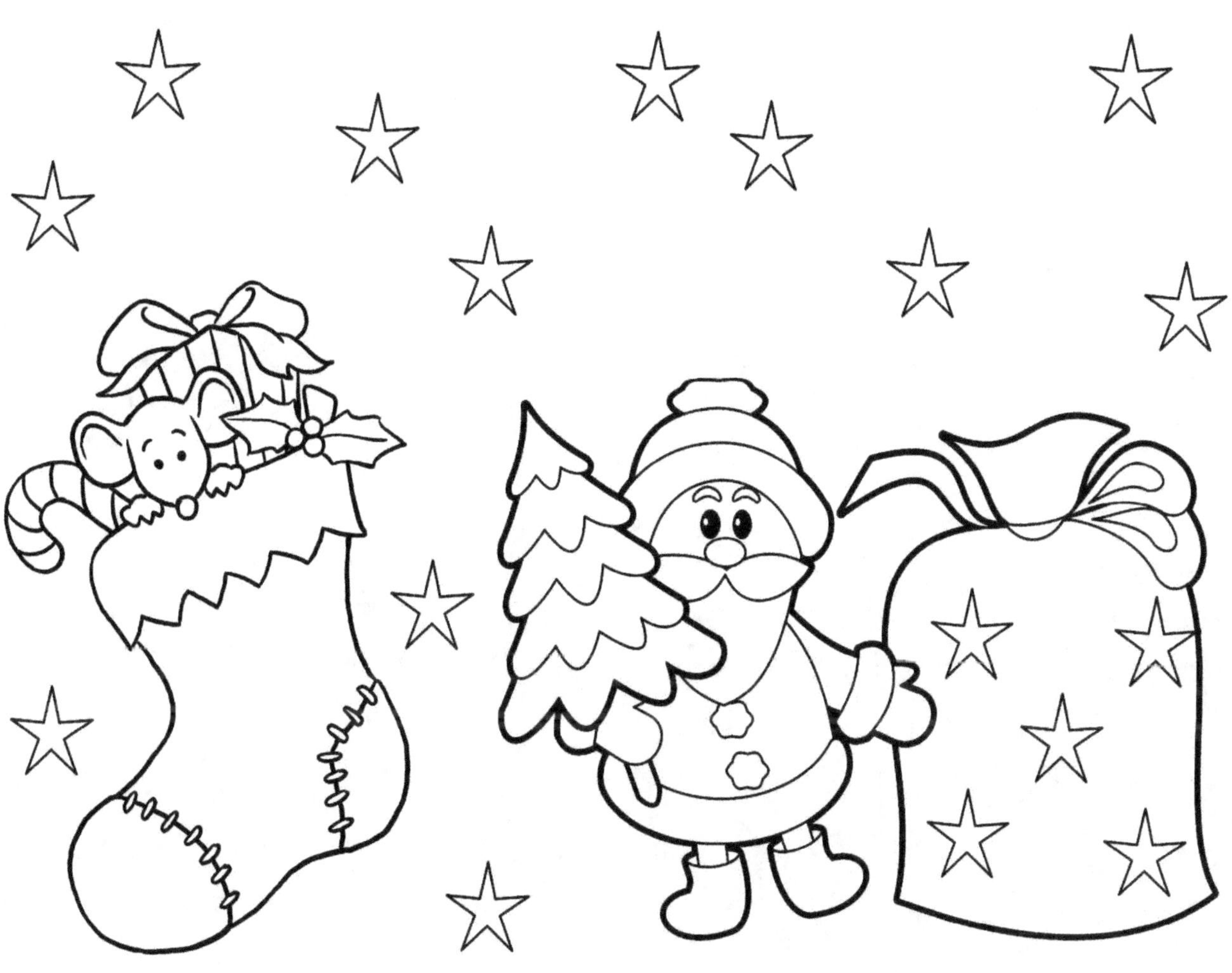

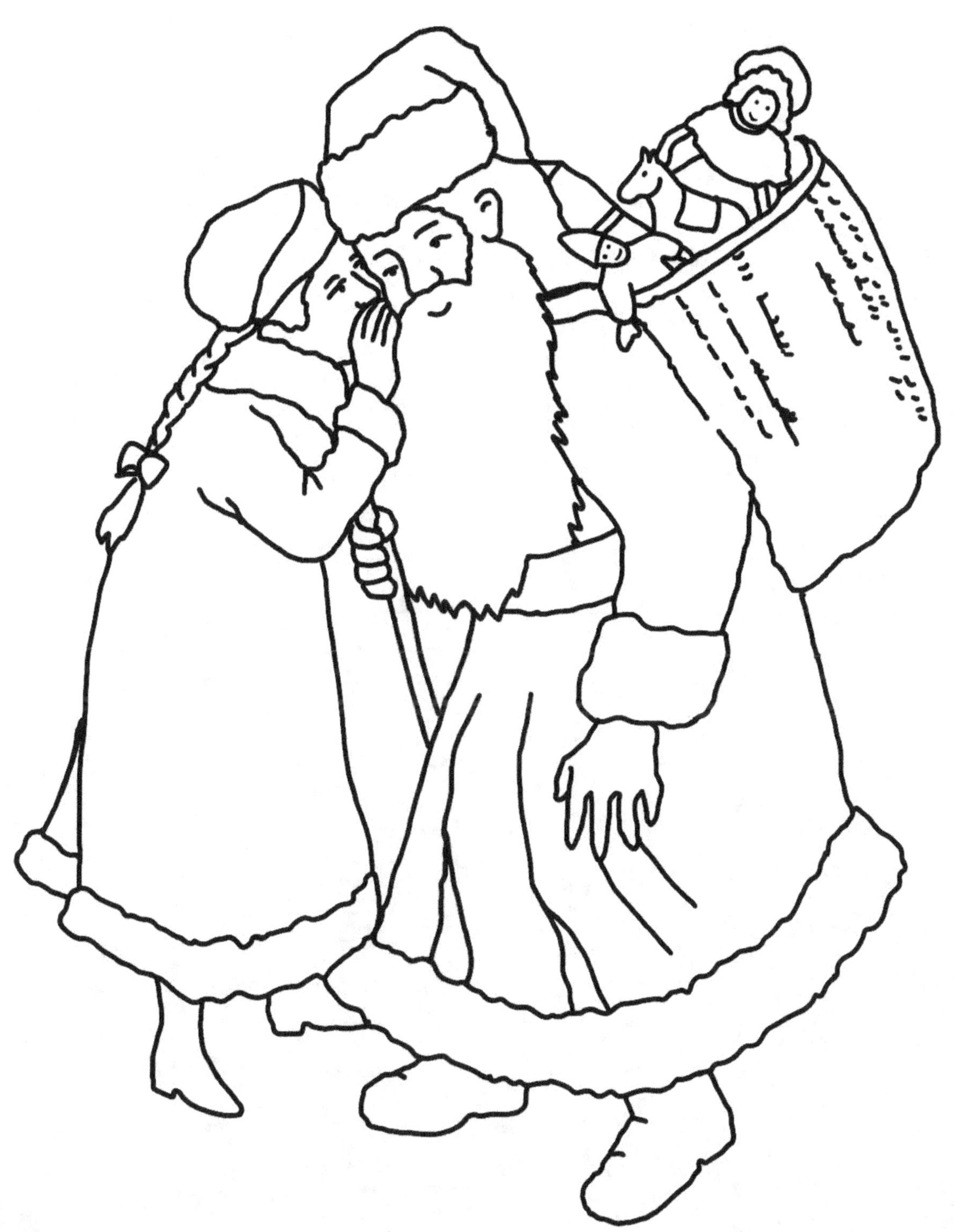

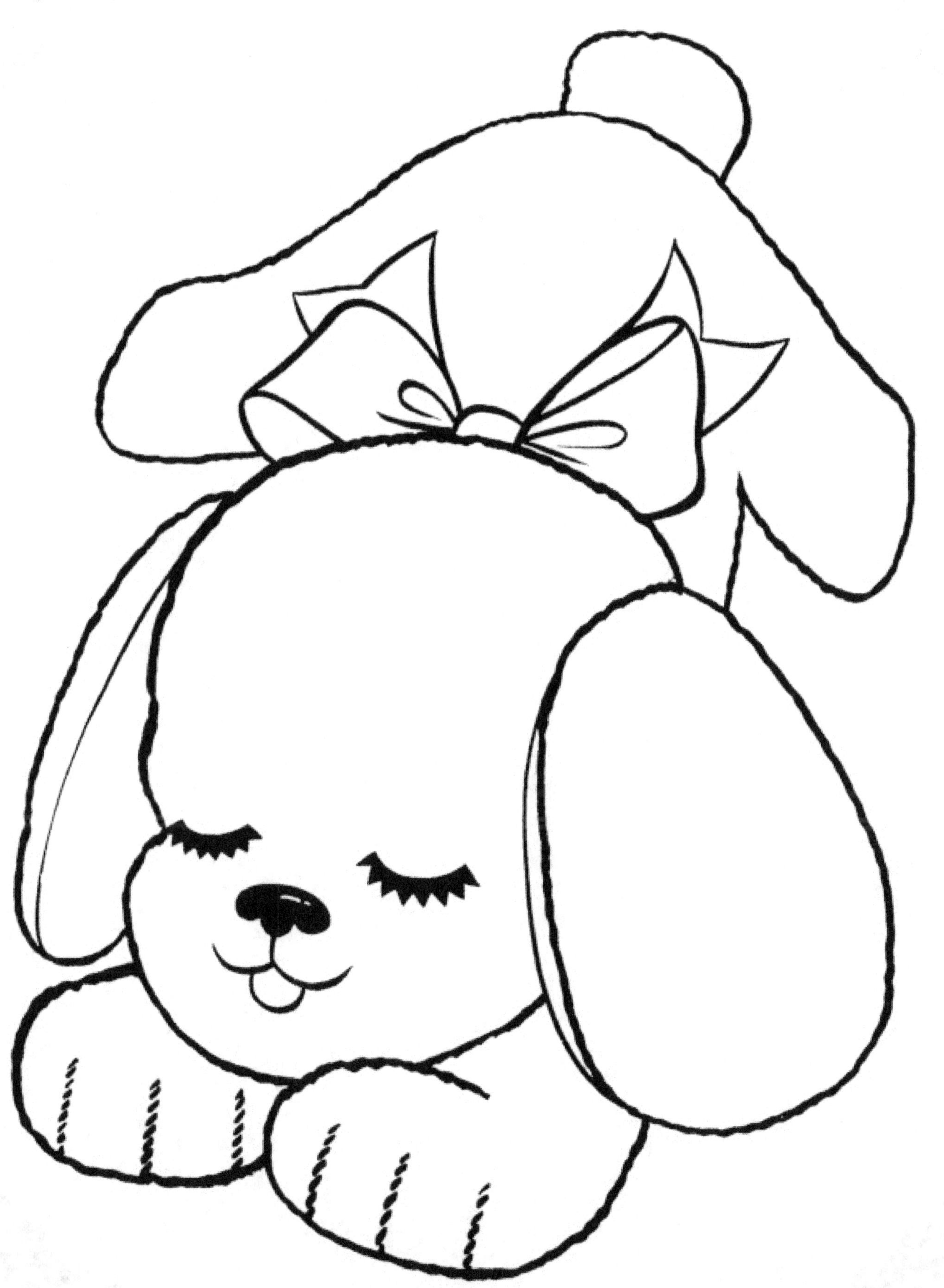

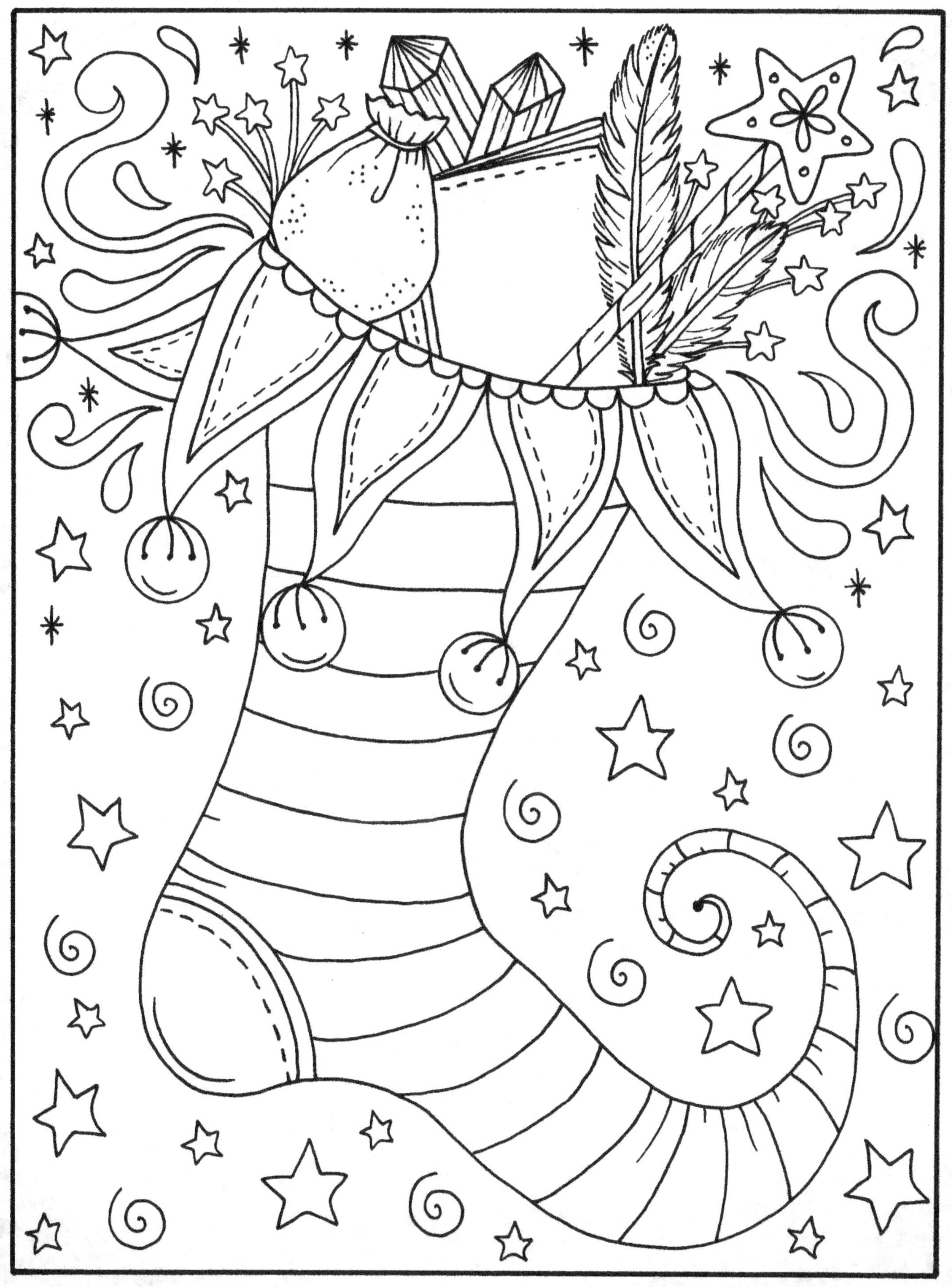

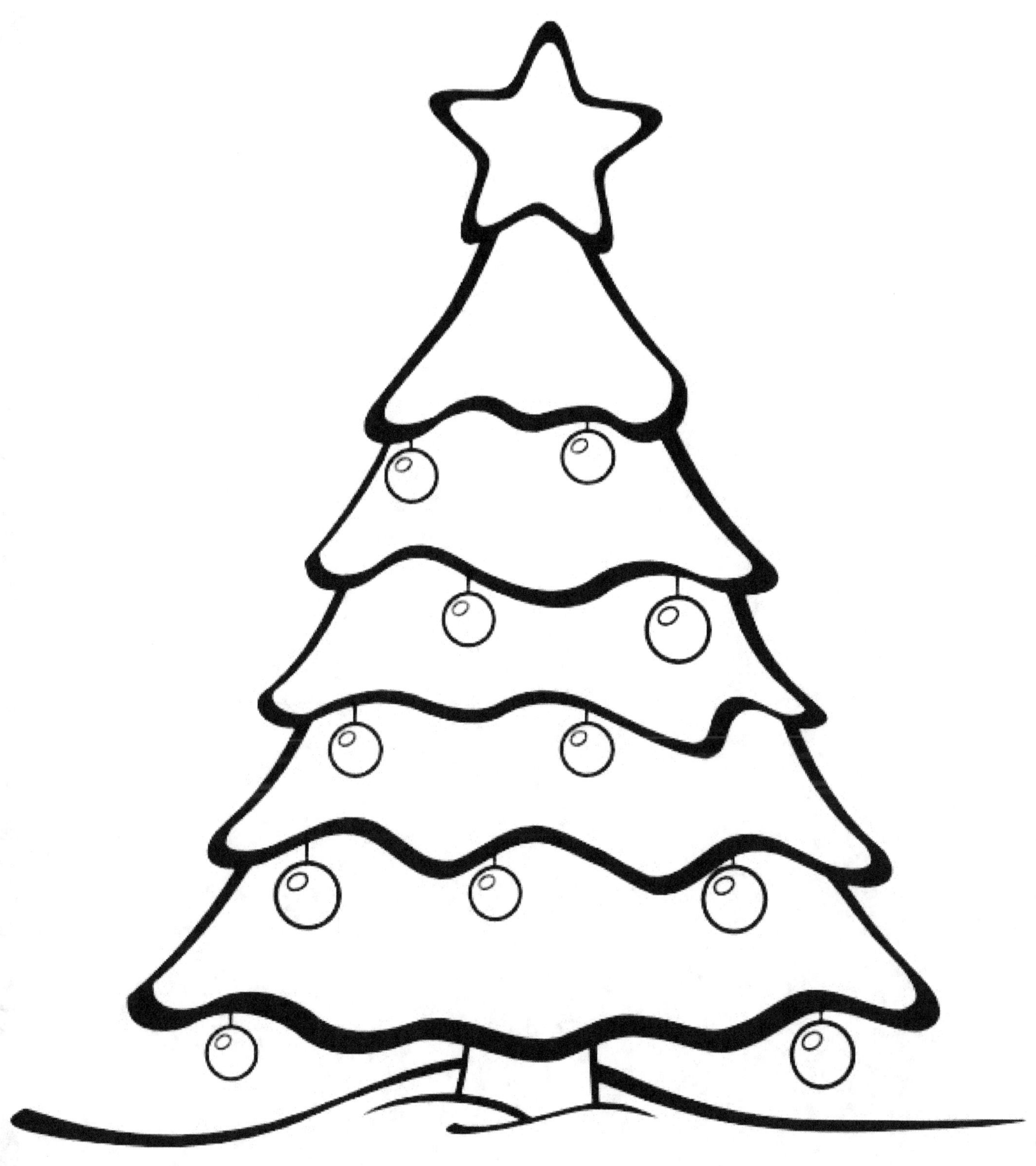

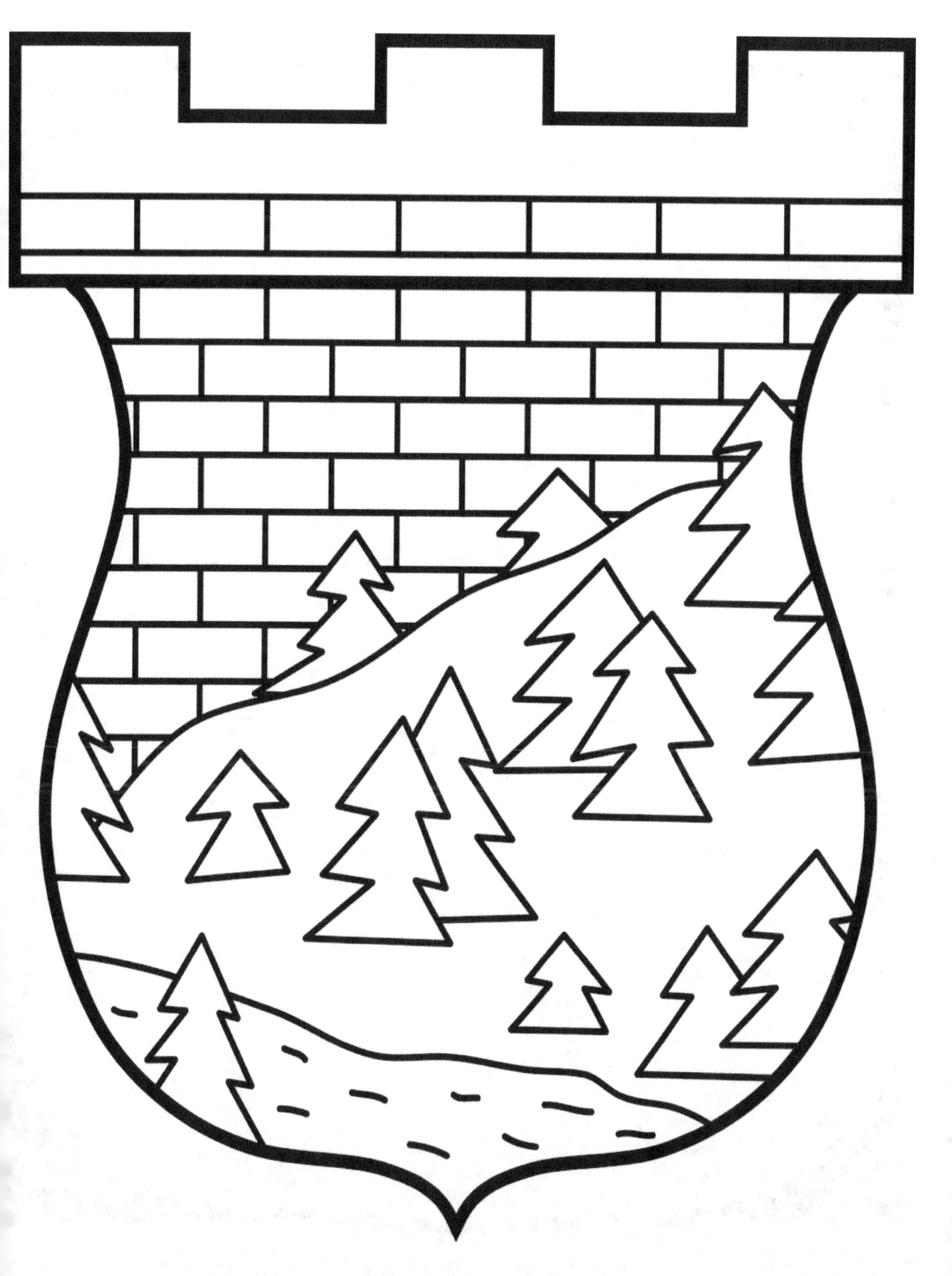

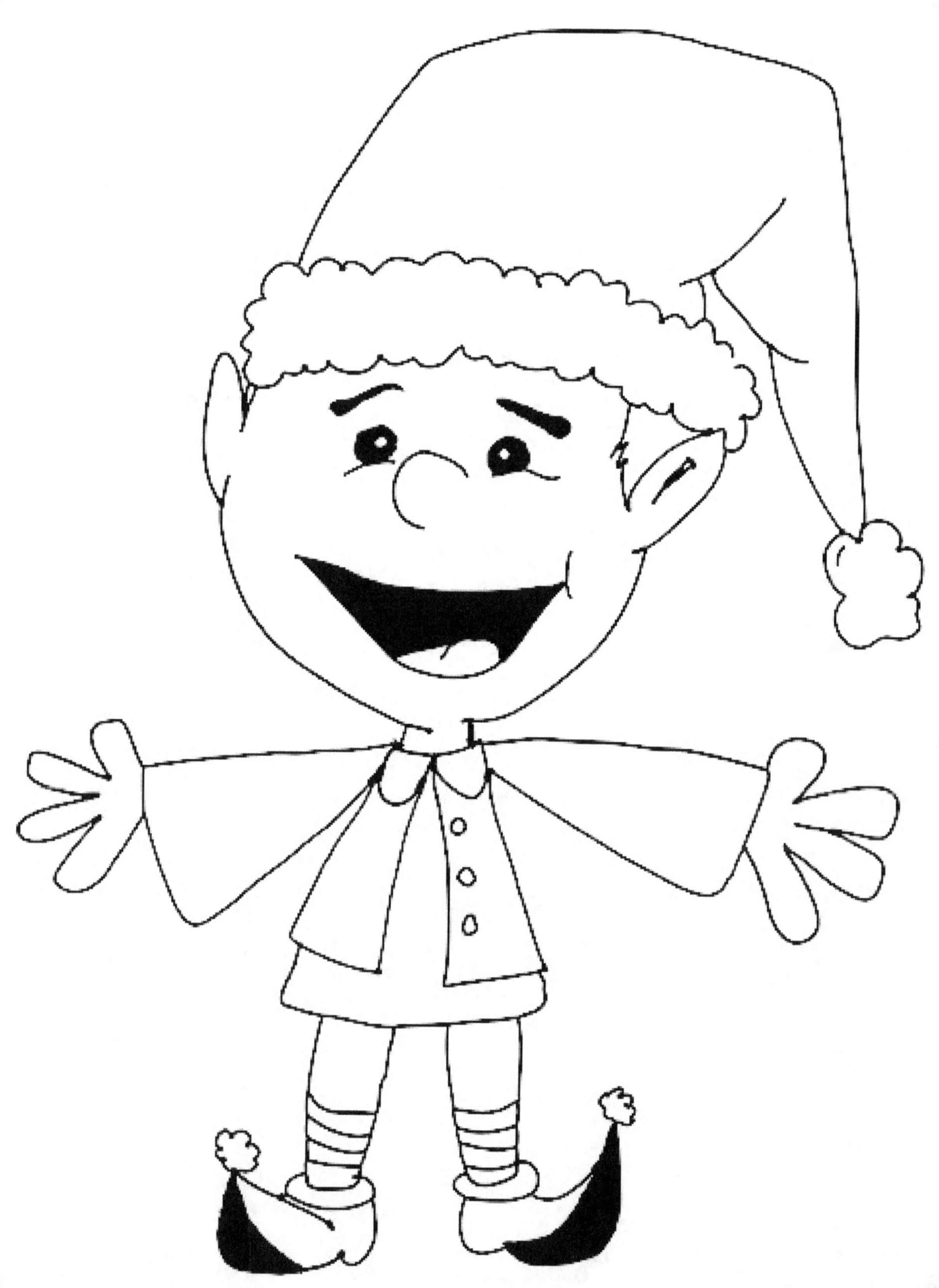

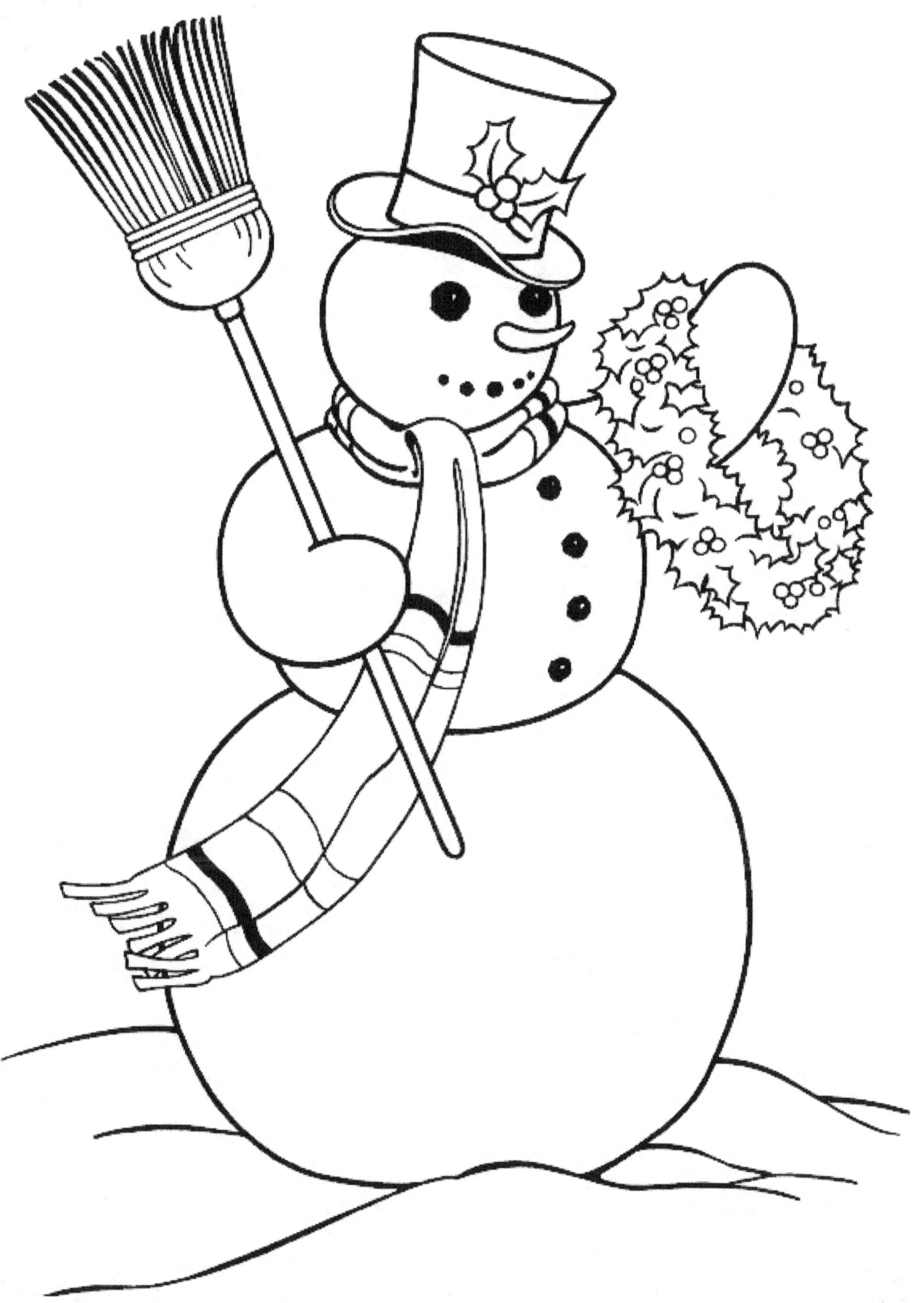

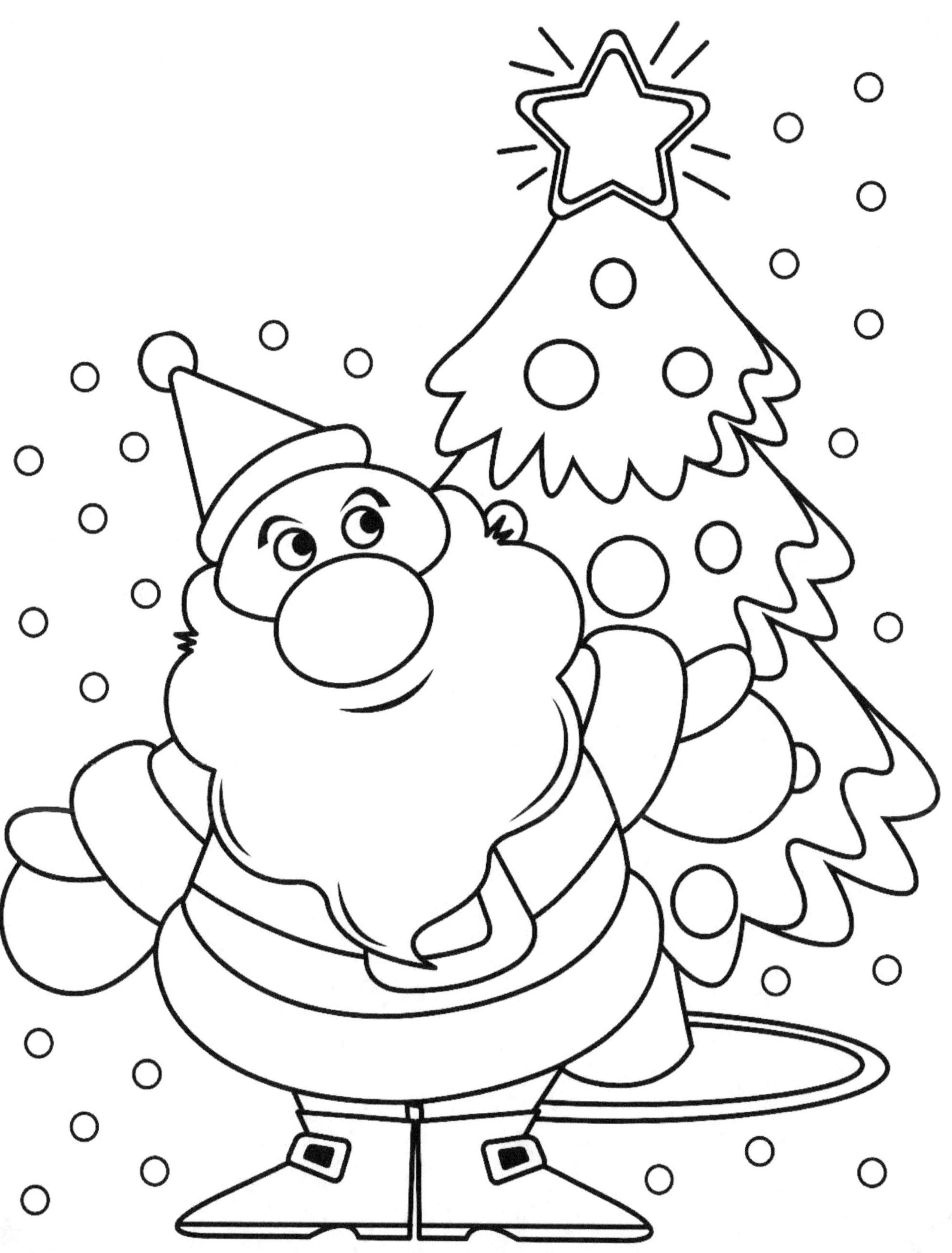

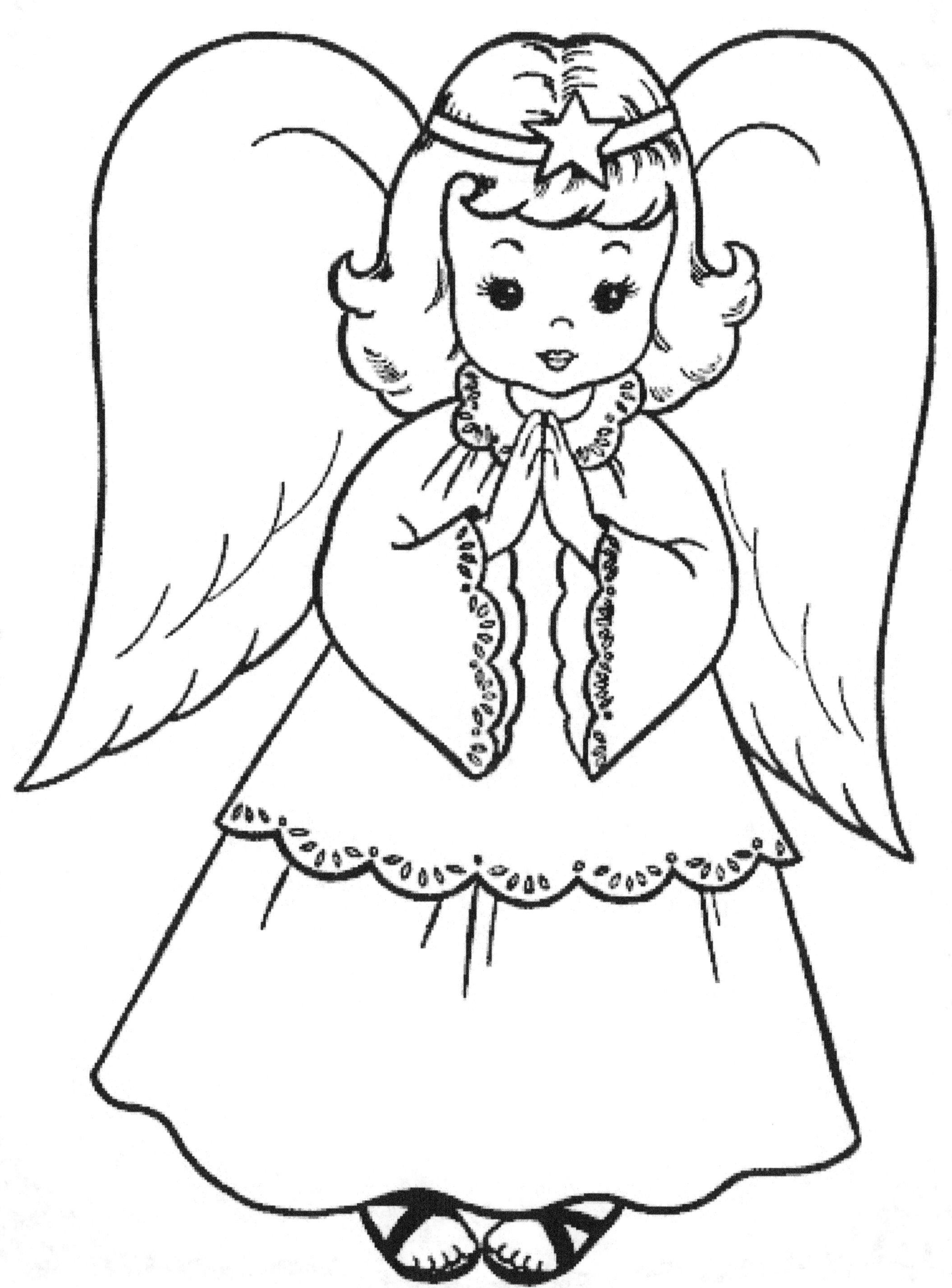